MOBILE SUIT GUNDAM SEED シード

>> ① <<

Original Story By
Hajime Yatate and Yoshiyuki Tomino

Written By
Liu Goto

Illustrated By
Tomofumi Ogasawara

TOKYOPOP®

HAMBURG // LONDON // LOS ANGELES // TOKYO

Mobile Suit Gundam SEED Vol 1
Original Story by: Hajime Yatate and Yoshiyuki Tomino
Written by: Liu Goto
Illustrated by: Tomofumi Ogasawara

Translation - Sue Shambaugh
English Adaptation - Joshua Arsenault and Kara Stambach
Associate Editor - Kara Stambach
Design and Layout - Jose Macasocol, Jr.
Cover Design - Louis Csontos

Editor - Nicole Monastirsky
Digital Imaging Manager - Chris Buford
Production Managers - Jennifer Miller and Mutsumi Miyazaki
Managing Editor - Jill Freshney
VP of Production - Ron Klamert
Publisher and E.I.C. - Mike Kiley
President and C.O.O. - John Parker
C.E.O. - Stuart Levy

A  Novel

TOKYOPOP Inc.
5900 Wilshire Blvd. Suite 2000
Los Angeles, CA 90036

E-mail: info@TOKYOPOP.com
Come visit us online at www.TOKYOPOP.com

Originally published in Japan as *MOBILE SUIT GUNDAM SEED, SURECHIGAU TSUBASA* © 2003 Liu GOTO © SOTSU AGENCY • SUNRISE • MBS First published in Japan in 2003 by KADOKAWA SHOTEN PUBLISHING CO., LTD., Tokyo. English translation rights arranged with KADOKAWA SHOTEN PUBLISHING CO., LTD., Tokyo through TUTTLE-MORI AGENCY, INC., Tokyo. English text copyright © 2005 TOKYOPOP Inc

ISBN: 1-59532-881-5

First TOKYOPOP printing: October 2005
10 9 8 7 6 5 4 3 2 1
Printed in Canada

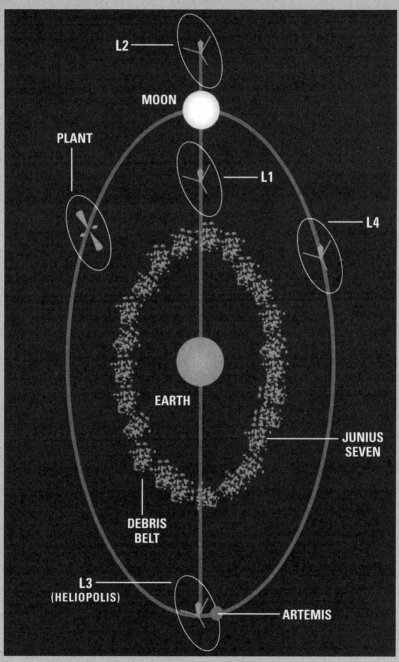

MOBILE SUIT GUNDAM SEED — SPACE AREA MAP CE 71

**MOBILE SUIT
GUNDAM SEED
ART GALLERY**
illustrated by TOMOFUMI OGASAWARA

GAT-X105 STRIKE & KIRA YAMATO

MOBILE SUIT GUNDAM SEED

>>1<<

THE YOUNG PEOPLE OF HELIOPOLIS:

Kira Yamato -

A student living in the neutral space colony of Heliopolis. Born with special talents, he pilots the X105 Strike.

Flay Allster -

A popular schoolgirl and the object of Kira's secret affection. Her father is the Undersecretary of the Atlantic Federation.

Tolle Koenig -

Kira's best friend and classmate at the Industrial College of Heliopolis. A friendly, fun-loving kid.

Miriallia Haw -
Tolle's girlfriend and Kira's classmate. Smart and chipper, her upbeat personality always cheers her friends.

Sai Argyle -
Kira's friend and classmate. He is an intellectual and often acts as a mediator for their group.

Kuzzey Buskirk -
A friend of the Heliopolis students. By comparing himself to Kira, he begins to doubt his own abilities.

Oppose Aggressors & Neutralize Invasion Enforcer

EARTH FEDERATION FORCE (SENIOR OFFICERS):

Murrue Ramius -
Atlantic Federation Lieutenant. She reluctantly takes command of the Archangel after its captain is killed in a ZAFT attack.

Natarle Badgiruel -
Atlantic Federation Ensign. A born soldier, she is a cold woman who always puts duty first.

Mu La Flaga -
Seventh Mobile Fleet Lieutenant. An ace pilot who operates the mobile armor Zero. Sarcastic and a bit of a playboy, he goes by the nickname, "the Hawk of Endymion."

Admiral Halberton -
Atlantic Federation Commodore and Eighth Fleet Admiral. He first proposed the development plan for the X series of mobile suits.

EARTH FEDERATION FORCE (PETTY OFFICERS):

Arnold Neumann -
He takes over as pilot of the Archangel when its crew is killed in a ZAFT attack.

Jackie Tonomura -
He is controller of the Archangel's Command Information Center (CIC).

Oppose Aggressors & Neutralize Invasion Enforcer

Oppose Aggressors & Neutralize Invasion Enforcer

Dalida Lolaha Chandra II - He is in charge of communications and data analysis for the Archangel's CIC.

Romero Pal -
He takes over duty as gunnery officer on the Archangel after its crew is killed.

Kojiro Murdoch -
He is in charge of maintenance for the Strike and Zero. A tough and hearty man, he is also extremely skillful and spirited.

ZAFT:

Rau Le Creuset -

The chilling ZAFT commander who hides his face behind a mask. He leads an elite team of pilots in pursuit of the Earth Force's secret weapons.

Athrun Zala -

An ace pilot on Creuset's team and a close childhood friend of Kira Yamato.

Lacus Clyne -

Athrun's fiancée and the daughter of PLANT Supreme Council Chairman Siegel Clyne.

Zodiac Alliance of Freedom Treaty

Zodiac Alliance of Freedom Treaty

Dearka Elsman -
An ace pilot on Creuset's team with a stubborn and cynical attitude.

Nicol Amalfi -
An ace pilot on Creuset's team. He has a low-key nature and is burdened with doubts about the war.

Yzak Joule -
An ace pilot on Creuset's team; his pride is matched only by his ambition.

GAT -X105 STRIKE GUNDAM

Overall height: 58 feet

Weight: 65 tons

Armament: 3-inch automatic multi-barrel CIWS, 2 Ingelstellungs, 2 assault knives, Armor Schneider, and 2 high-energy beam rifles.

Pilot: Kira Yamato

One of the five Earth Alliance prototypes developed secretly on Heliopolis, the Strike Gundam is equipped with Phase Shift Armor and anti-beam coating to protect it from physical combat and high-energy weaponry. Using different Striker Packs, (weapons modules with backup batteries) the mobile suit can recharge and re-adapt to a variety of combat situations. With young Coordinator Kira Yamato at the controls, the Strike's performance exceeds all expectations.

AILE FORM

Aile Strike

The Aile Strike Gundam has power vernier thrusters for superb mobility in the atmosphere and space. It includes a beam rifle and beam sabers for medium- and close-range combat. It is the Strike's most versatile form.

Overall height: 58 feet

Weight: 85 tons

Armament: 2 beam sabers and a pair of 3-inch high-energy beam rifles.

Oppose Aggressors & Neutralize Invasion Enforcer

GAT-X105 STRIKE GUNDAM

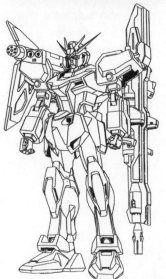

LAUNCHER FORM

Launcher Strike Gundam

The Launcher Striker pack contains a battery of medium- and long-range weapons, including a hyper impulse cannon with firepower equal to that of several warships combined.

Overall height: 58 feet

Weight: 84 tons

Armament: 2 combo weapons pods (4.7-inch anti-ship vulcan cannon, 13.7-inch gun launcher), and Agni, the 13.7-inch hyper impulse canon.

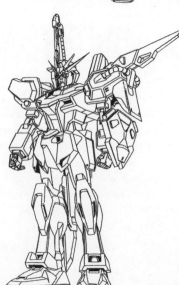

SWORD FORM

Sword Strike Gundam

Designed for close-range combat, the Sword Striker has an anti-ship laser blade and a beam boomerang, as well as a small shield on its forearm, coupled with a grappling device that can be launched at enemy machines.

Overall height: 58 feet

Weight: 74 tons

Armament: 2 beam boomerangs called Midas Messer and a rocket anchor called Panzer Eisen, plus the Schwert Gewehr, a 52-foot anti-ship blade.

GAT-X303
AEGIS GUNDAM

One of the four prototypes stolen by ZAFT. Its X300-series frame allows it to transform into a clawed mobile armor in order to seize and destroy enemy mobile suits. It carries a beam rifle and an anti-beam coated shield. The Aegis was meant to serve as a command unit, watching over the other GAT-X Numbers.

AEGIS

Overall height: 62 feet
Weight: 80 tons
Armament: 3-inch automatic multi-barrel CIWS, 2 Igelstellungs, 2 beam sabers, 4 high-energy beam rifles and a multi-phase energy cannon "Scylla" when in mobile armor form.
Pilot: Athrun Zala

Zodiac Alliance of Freedom Treaty

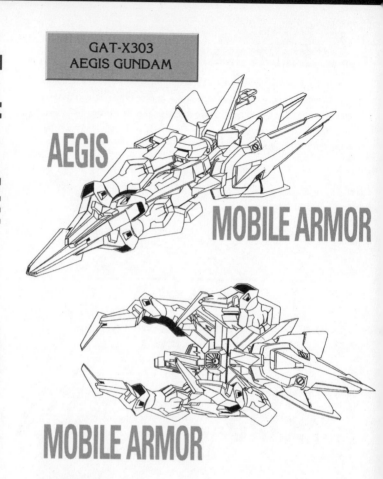

GAT-X303
AEGIS GUNDAM

AEGIS

MOBILE ARMOR

MOBILE ARMOR

Mobile Armor

Mass-produced machines, also known as Moebiuses, that form the backbone of the Earth Alliance space forces. They can be equipped with missiles and heavy weapons in addition to a built-in pair of vulcan canons and a standard linear gun capable of destroying a mobile suit or the hull armor of a warship. Its performance is still inferior to a Gundam, however.

GAT-X102 DUEL

One of the four stolen prototypes, the Duel is the earliest and most orthodox of the X Numbers. This general-purpose machine served as the base model to develop the more specialized Buster and Strike. It is armed with a beam rifle, two beam sabers, and carries an anti-beam coated shield.

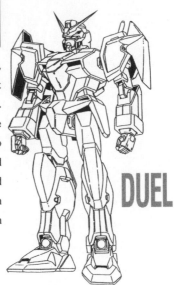

DUEL

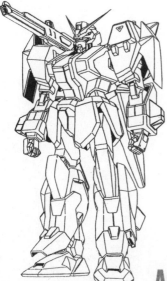

Overall height: 57.5 feet
Weight: 62 tons
Armament: 3-inch automatic multi-barrel CIWS, 2 Igelstellungs, 2 beam sabers, 2 high-energy beam files, 7-inch grenade launchers.
Pilot: Yzak Joule

ASSAULT MODE

Zodiac Alliance of Freedom Treaty

Zodiac Alliance of Freedom Treaty

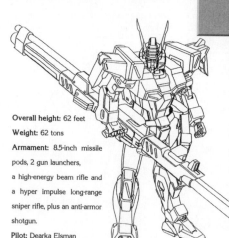

GAT-X103 BUSTER

One of the four stolen prototypes, the Buster is designed for medium- and long-range attacks, intended to provide flank support by bombarding enemy warships and bases from long distances. The Buster's beam rifle and gun launcher combine to form a long-range sniper rifle or shotgun-style scattering weapon. Its shoulder missile pods can shoot enemies at close range.

Overall height: 62 feet

Weight: 62 tons

Armament: 8.5-inch missile pods, 2 gun launchers, a high-energy beam rifle and a hyper impulse long-range sniper rifle, plus an anti-armor shotgun.

Pilot: Dearka Elsman

BUSTER

GAT-X207 BLITZ

One of the four stolen prototypes, its X200-series frame is designed to support special weapons, the Mirage Colloid system in particular, which renders the mobile suit invisible to radar, infra-red sensors, and the naked eye. Its stealth makes it perfect for infiltrating enemy territory; its rocket-propelled grappling claw and Trikeros shield system enable it to carry out surprise attacks.

Overall height: 61 feet

Weight: 73.5 tons

Armament: piercer lock Gleipnir, offensive shield system Trikeros, a high-energy beam rifle, a beam saver, and 3 hyper-fast kinetic energy penetrators called Lancer Dart.

Pilot: Nicol Amalfi

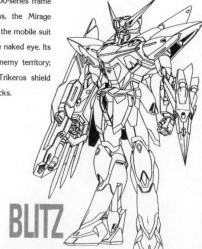

BLITZ

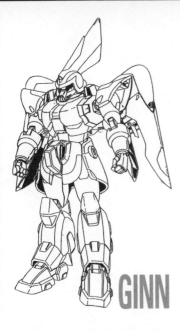

GINN

GINN

The first combat mobile suit and the backbone of ZAFT military forces. One GINN equals five mobile armors. They can single-handedly destroy an Earth Force escort ship. Classified as a Zero Gravity Maneuver Fighter, its versatility ensures it can operate in a variety of Earth environments as well as space. A machine gun and a blade for slicing apart enemy mobile armors complete its standard armament, but the GINN can also be outfitted with a variety of guided missiles and heavy weapons.

Overall height: 70 feet

Weight: 78.5 tons

Armament: MMI-M8A3 heavy assault machine gun, MA-M3 heavy blade, M66 Canis short-range guided missile launcher, M68 Pardus short-range guided missile launcher, M69 Barrus heavy ion cannon, M68 Cattus recoilless rifle.

CGUE

Designed in the early days of the war as a replacement for the mass-produced GINN, the CGUE has higher mobility than its predecessor and is equipped with new and improved weapons, including a built-in vulcan cannon in the shield on its left arm. Because the CGUE never reached the mass production stage, the few units that were developed have been assigned to commanders like Rau Le Creuset.

Overall height: 70 feet

Weight: 80.22 tons

Armament: MMI-M7S heavy assault machine gun, MA-M4A heavy blade, M7070 vulcan system shield.

CGUE

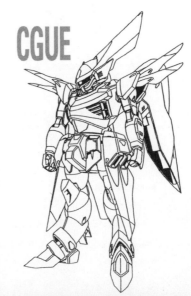

Zodiac Alliance of Freedom Treaty

Oppose Aggressors & Neutralize Invasion Enforcer

ASSAULT MOVEMENT
SPECIAL EQUIPMENT WARSHIP
ARCHANGEL

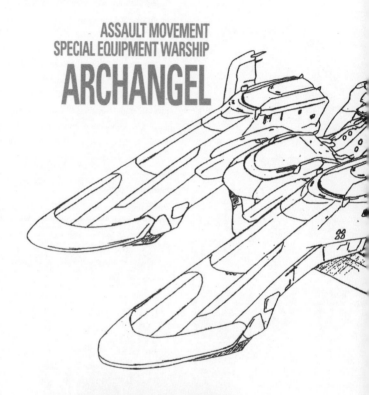

ARCHANGEL

Constructed by the Atlantic Federation in secrecy, this custom-built mobile assault ship is designed to support the prototype Gundams with a variety of powerful weapons and experimental systems, including laminated armor, which protects it from enemy beam weapons, and ablative gel dispensers, that allow it to survive atmospheric entry. Extensively automated, the Archangel can be operated by a small crew.

Overall length: 1132 feet

Armament: dual high-energy beam cannon, 2 Gottfried Mk.71s, 2 linear canons called Valiant Mk8, 2 positron blaster canons called Lohengrins, 16 automatic multi-barrel CIWS Igelstellungs, 24 large missile launchers, 16 surface-to-air missile launchers, and several anti-beam depth charge launchers.

Oppose Aggressors & Neutralize Invasion Enforcer

Oppose Aggressors & Neutralize Invasion Enforcer

MOEBUIS ⟨ZERO⟩

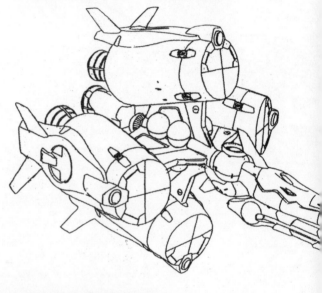

MOEBIUS ZERO

An Earth Alliance special forces mobile armor that served as the basis for the mass-produced Moebius. Equipped with the standard linear gun and a set of four wire-guided gun barrels, the Zero can overwhelm enemy mobile suits with a simultaneous multi-directional attack.

GUN BARREL OF WIRE SYSTEM

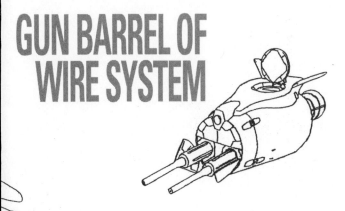

GUN BARREL
WIRE SYSTEM

One of the few pilots capable of operating these gun barrels, Mu La Flaga earned the nickname "the Hawk of Endymion" by using his Moebius Zero to destroy five GINNS on the lunar surface.

Cosmic Era 30:

Breakthroughs in genetic engineering peak. An advanced race of humans called Coordinators are created. They surpass unaltered humans (Naturals) in every aspect—strength, intelligence, and creativity.

Resented and feared for their extraordinary abilities, the Coordinators are driven from their homes on Earth. They seek peace in the only place left to them—the vast coldness of space.

Cosmic Era 50:

Earth suffers a devastating energy crisis. Extraterrestrial industrial centers called PLANTs (Productive Location Ally on Nexus Technology) are built as a means of obtaining energy from interstellar resources.

Coordinators labor in the PLANT colonies, but are unable to share the profits of these celestial strongholds. Forbidden *to produce any weaponry, or to even grow their own food, the Coordinators are totally dependent on the superpower countries of Earth.*

Cosmic Era 70:

The Coordinators rebel. Peace talks prove futile. Tensions between Coordinators and Naturals reach epic proportions. Fighting breaks out.

Three days after war is declared, (on February 14, CE 70) the Earth Alliance launches a sneak attack on the Coordinator PLANT Junius Seven – the only station capable of harvesting agriculture and feeding the rest of Coordinator territory. Nuclear missiles (stashed aboard the mobile armor carrier Roosevelt) decimate the Junius Seven; over two hundred and forty-three thousand people are massacred in an instant.

Nicknamed the Bloody Valentine, this tragedy becomes a call to arms for young Coordinators, who rush to join the ZAFT (Zodiac Alliance of Freedom Treaty) Army. Although the Coordinators are few in number compared to the Naturals, their special abilities and enhanced technology make them formidable opponents. The war quickly reaches a stalemate. Eleven months of intense fighting pass . . .

> > > > >

Industrial College, Heliopolis:

"There are reports of fierce fighting on the South China front. Last week the ZAFT Army closed in just three and a half miles from the spaceport. More news when we return."

Kira Yamato's wandering gaze shifted to his laptop. A quick jab at the keys with his forefinger and the news window closed. He was sick of hearing about the war.

Relatively slight for his age, Kira's slender face made him seem younger than his sixteen years. With jet-black hair and dark eyes, he could easily have passed for a person of Asian decent. Quiet and somewhat shy, he kept to himself most of the time. Today, he sat alone at a picnic table situated squarely in the grassy quad.

Sunlight filtered through the trees. Around him, students were laughing, strolling, studying. By all accounts, it was a typical college scene. Except this was Heliopolis, a space colony located at L3 in orbit far above Earth. Beneath the bright green turf was an alloy frame three hundred and thirty feet thick, and below that, the vacuum of space. Heliopolis itself was fifteen miles long and two miles wide, powered by solar mirrors on its surface that resembled long, thin petals of glass.

Birdy, a gold and emerald robo-pet, swooped around Kira's head and perched atop his computer. "Toro!" it chirped cheerfully.

Kira smiled at his treasured pet. Whenever he looked at Birdy, it reminded him of the boy who built it . . .

Earth's moon, four years earlier:

Young Kira stared up at his best friend, Athrun Zala, for perhaps the last time. He fought back tears.

"I think Father worries too much," Athrun said quietly, his voice soft and self-assured. It calmed Kira somewhat. "There won't be a war between the PLANTs and Earth."

Kira, lost in Athrun's emerald green eyes, nodded solemnly. He trusted Athrun.

His friend sighed. "But they told us to evacuate anyway, so we have to go."

Kira looked down. Athrun and his family were Coordinators. Kira's parents were Naturals. Although he didn't understand the political reasons, he knew that their separation was inevitable.

"Don't worry," Athrun encouraged. "You'll go to a PLANT soon, too." Kira looked up into those big green eyes and smiled. "Besides, I'm sure we'll meet again."

"Yo. Any breaking news?"

Kira startled as Tolle Koenig squeezed into the seat beside him and peeked at his computer screen.

"Hey, Tolle," Kira greeted.

Tolle's girlfriend, Miriallia Haw, leaned over the taller boy's shoulder. Kira pulled up the news screen and the three of them watched as black smoke rose from large explosions, mobs of people fled through the streets, and rows of buildings lay in waste. The battle played out far below on Earth, but these pictures made it somehow seem very close.

Last year the ZAFT Army started invading Earth from the PLANT colonies. Everyone on Heliopolis—a neutral territory—waited with baited breath as the conflict unfolded on the news. But ZAFT and the Earth Alliance had been in a stalemate for so long, people had grown accustomed to the hostilities.

A field reporter shouted into his microphone, "Here at point-four miles from South China, you can hear the sounds of destruction!"

"Oh boy," Tolle said sarcastically. "Only a week and already China's falling?"

Kira liked Tolle (despite finding him sometimes annoying) and appreciated the boy's honest, shoot-from-the-hip demeanor. Plus, Tolle and Miriallia were always fun to be around, in or out of class. They were his closest friends here on Heliopolis.

Miriallia asked nervously, "Isn't South China sorta close? You think we'll be okay?"

"Sure," Tolle shrugged. "This place'll never become a war zone."

Tolle's optimistic outlook reminded Kira of Athrun. But Athrun had been wrong . . .

> > > > >

"It's not true!"

Kira's head snapped up as he and his friends approached the elecar rental platform. A group of girls clustered around Flay Allster, a beautiful young lady with fire-engine-red hair, a petite frame, and the poise of a ballerina. She stood out from other girls like an exotic bloom among common flowers. On the rare occasions when she spoke to him, Kira's stomach always did flip-flops.

Kira watched Flay blush under the girls' intense prying. His pulse quickened as their eyes met.

"Hey, Miriallia!" one of the girls called. "You know, don't you?"

Flay stomped her foot. "Enough already!"

"Know what?" Miriallia asked.

"Flay got a love letter . . . from Sai Argyle!" the girl said with glee. "And she says it's no big deal. But she won't even talk about him!"

"Ehhh?! Really?" Miriallia gasped over the chatter.

A calm voice cut through the chaos. "If you're not going to move on, may we pass?"

The students spun around to see a sophisticated woman with a severe haircut. Two taller and equally imposing men waited patiently behind her. The woman looked as if she was in her mid-twenties, certainly not a student; her words were polite, but she carried herself with a distinctly professional air. She was a tad intimidating.

"Y-yeah, sorry," Kira apologized. "Go ahead."

Tolle hung his head and awkwardly stepped aside. The three adults got in the next available elecar and sped away. Kira watched them go with a sense of foreboding.

Flay and her girlfriends grabbed the following car, leaving Kira and his friends alone on the ramp.

Tolle clapped him on the shoulder. "Well, that's a shocking bit of news, isn't it, buddy? A love letter from Sai? Seems you've got a rival for the lady's affections!"

"Huh? Wh-what?" Kira stammered.

Miriallia smiled. "Don't give up!" She and Tolle hopped into the elecar.

"W-wait. It's not like that," Kira mumbled. He slumped into the backseat.

> > > > >

Natarle Badgiruel adjusted her sunglasses and stared at the scenery as the elecar whizzed toward the colony's Central Shaft. Her short black hair ruffled in the wind. She frowned, thinking of the students she'd seen on the platform. She couldn't believe there were kids that age already on the front lines.

As an ensign lieutenant in the Earth Alliance, Natarle had witnessed many horrible battles on Earth; seeing the stark contrast of the peaceful shops and homes of Heliopolis felt perverse. Arnold Neumann, Chief Petty Officer, must have sensed her exasperation, but they both knew this visit to Heliopolis was vital to their mission.

As one of the industrial colonies for the neutral nation of Orb, (a group of Pacific Islands just below the equator) Heliopolis was a pipeline of interstellar raw materials to Earth. As the war dragged on, various nations took sides, allying themselves with either Coordinators or Naturals. Outwardly, Orb refused to become embroiled with the conflict. That was why the Earth Alliance officers' arrival needed to remain a secret.

The automatic elecar descended into the Central Shaft. As gravity diminished, stray pieces of trash danced around them. The Central Shaft formed the backbone of Heliopolis; axial shafts connected it to the inner wall, like vertebrae attaching to a spine. People used the axial shafts to travel around the cylindrical-shaped colony, but the shafts also served to support the colony's outer shell, which constantly rotated to create gravity. In other words, the Central Shaft acted like a planet's axis.

Deep inside the Central Shaft was the factory district. The entire area was at zero gravity; products were manufactured efficiently in weightless conditions. On one side of the shaft was a spaceport; on the other, an asteroid mine, abundant with raw materials. The elecar zoomed toward the asteroid.

Morgenroete, a government-owned business, mined massive caverns deep into the asteroid. The elecar docked at a hanger in one of these caverns. Natarle and the two men floated over to an observation platform that jutted out of the asteroid—they leaned over the railing on a huge precipice—and saw it at last: a gleaming white battleship.

Its length spanned more than three football fields. On both sides of the main section, gunwales extended like the forelimbs of a crouching beast. Wings spread out of the central body—it could fly through the atmosphere as well as space. Its massive body armor made it look like a fortress.

This was the Archangel, a new battleship the Earth Alliance Force had been secretly constructing within the confines of Morgenroete. Ensign Lieutenant Natarle Badgiruel,

Chief Petty Officer Arnold Neumann, and Petty Officer Jack Tonomura were soldiers in the Earth Force's Eighth Fleet—they had come to Heliopolis in order to board the Archangel as crewmembers.

Surely this new ship would be the answer to all their prayers and bring a swift end to the deadlocked war.

> > > > >

Kira and his friends took the elecar inside Morgenroete's Industrial Complex for a routine visit to Professor Kato's lab. Their Industrial College was intricately connected to the commercial activities of Morgenroete, and whether they realized it or not, this put them smack-dab in the middle of the war.

The students trained with top-level mechanical engineers and physicists, such as Professor Kato, who tutored them about cutting-edge technology. In return, the students worked on projects, completely unaware of how Morgenroete put their work to use.

As they entered the lab, Sai raised his head from his microscope. "Hey, you guys finally made it!" he said happily. Sai was a mature, serious person, despite his outrageous fashion sense. Today he wore tinted glasses and a loud, tacky jacket. A year older than the rest of them, Sai often found himself playing mediator for his hot-tempered friends.

Kuzzey Buskirk, another classmate, sat at the table at the far end of the room. Next to him was a smaller student whom Kira had never seen before. A hat obscured the stranger's face.

"Who's that?" Tolle asked Kuzzey.

Kuzzey shrugged. "A guest of the professor, I guess. He said he was supposed to wait here."

Kira eyed the newcomer. Golden hair jutted out from under the hat. His limbs were slender, like a child's. What did this little kid have to do with Professor Kato, the cybernetic engineering genius?

Sai held up a disc for Kira. "I was supposed to give this to you. Professor Kato said you'd understand when you saw it. What is it, another supplement?"

"Oh, man!" Kira whined. "I haven't even finished with my other projects!"

For several months now, Kira had been assisting Professor Kato in his research. Though Kira was a mere student, the professor insisted that he processed data faster than any other student. Kira appreciated his teacher's special attention, but he didn't need the additional workload. Exasperated, Kira took the disc.

Tolle grabbed him from behind, putting him a loose headlock. "Never mind this stuff! What about the love letter, Sai?"

Kira's eyes bulged. He put his hand over Tolle's mouth and smiled at Sai. "I-it's nothing! Nothing!"

Flay was certainly beautiful, but Kira wasn't brave enough to confess his feelings for her just yet. If Sai made a move, he supposed he'd have to say something, but . . .

Kuzzey nudged Tolle. "What is it? Come on, tell us, tell us!"

Kira suddenly sensed eyes on him. The newcomer was glaring at them—those eyes an astonishingly sharp brown-gold. His face was delicate but his expression was harsh. Kira couldn't tear his eyes away.

> > > > >

Athrun Zala approached the asteroid of Heliopolis in stealth. He and his nine ZAFT team members, dressed alike in airtight spacesuits, snuck into a large exhaust port. Athrun calmly looked at his watch.

Beep.

The monitoring device on the exhaust port suddenly cut off—right on cue. Athrun gave the signal and his team slid inside the shaft, scattered silently to a strategic location, and planted a small black box.

Athrun carefully set his timer. The pulsing light from the display panel reflected in his green eyes.

> > > > >

Concealed behind the asteroid, two ZAFT battleships stood by. One was a Nazca-class ship, the Vesalius, and the other, a Laurasia-class transporter, called the Gamow. On the bridge of Vesalius, Captain Ades looked down upon Heliopolis with a concerned expression.

"Don't look so serious, Ades," his mysterious companion said. The captain's frown deepened. The superior officer beside him wore a green mask that concealed half his face—it was impossible to read his moods.

Commander Rau Le Creuset, known to his enemies and allies alike for his ferocious fighting abilities, had long, wavy blond hair and a square chin. Even with the mask, he looked rather dashing in comparison to Captain Ades.

The captain sighed. "There is still time to get an answer from the Supreme Council, Commander," he pressed.

Creuset shook his head. "It will take too long. My intuition tells me that if we don't act now . . . we'll die." Creuset's docile voice as he prophesied their death sent a shiver up Captain Ades' spine. "And as you know, my intuition is never wrong."

He watched as Creuset glanced at a fuzzy satellite photograph in his hand. It was a blurry image, but he could still make out the picture of a huge humanoid machine. "We'll steal the Earth Alliance Force's new super weapons before they even know what hit them."

> > > > >

The Morgenroete asteroid's construction site bustled with activity. Lieutenant Murrue Ramius, twenty-six, barked orders from her passing trailer tank. Although she was the highest-ranking officer on the site, her subordinates usually saluted her with woof-whistles and pickup lines.

"Lieutenant!"

She turned to see her mechanic, Petty Officer Murdoch, stick his gruff, unshaven face out of the window and shout, "We're going ahead to the ship!"

"Roger that!" she shouted back.

"Hey, Lieutenant, later, what do you say we go out for a drink? It's our last night on Heliopolis!" a young officer called out.

She raised a sardonic eyebrow. "I've got a better idea. How about *I* go out for a drink, and *you* can spend your last night in the brig for insulting a superior officer?"

Petty Officer Hamana laughed beside her. "Dummy," he chuckled to the young man. "You're too young to even think about Lieutenant Ramius. Try waiting about ten years."

Everyone's spirits were certainly high, Murrue thought, what with Operation G coming to a close. All they had to do was load this new weapon onto the Archangel for fine-tuning and their mission would be complete. Finally, the burden of command would be off Murrue's shoulders . . .

> > > > >

The two ZAFT battleships had been detected.

"Calling approaching ZAFT vessels! You are in severe violation of your treaty with Orb! Stop your ships at once!" a communications officer ordered over the intercom.

Senior officers hurried inside the control room above the Archangel's docking bay as personnel worked frantically to prepare for battle. Suddenly, all communication channels spat out deafening white noise.

An operator called out, "Strong electronic wave interference—it's coming from the ZAFT ships!"

A chill swept through the room.

The senior officer made the call. "Hostile intent, for certain."

Just then, a freighter the size of a small building sped into port. From its bridge, Lieutenant Mu La Flaga radioed into the control tower. His voice came in clearly despite the grating interference. "The enemy?"

"Two ships," the communications officer replied. "ZAFT. One was a Nazca-class and the other a Laurasia-class. Just before the wave interference hit, we confirmed the launch of mobile suits."

"What about the recruits?" La Flaga asked immediately.

"They've arrived and should be ready to board."

"At least that's one blessing," he said. "Don't depart without me—I'm headed to the Zero right now!"

La Flaga was a slim, blond man in his late twenties. His roughly handsome features belied a fiercely commanding presence. As the star pilot of the Earth Alliance Force, his bravery was renowned.

His freighter zoomed into the hangar bay where the mobile armors were lined up. The Earth Alliance had boasted an overwhelming number of these single-pilot space cruisers. Although powerful weapons in and of themselves, they rarely served as a match for the ZAFT humanoid mobile suits.

Mobile suits were designed specifically for the abilities of their Coordinator pilots. With propulsion wings sprouting from their backs, they nimbly operated in space or on land; the war hinged on the firepower of these modern weapons.

As La Flaga's freighter approached the mobile armors, a garbled radio message patched through. "Mobile suits have infiltrated the harbor entrance! We can't hold them! There are two coming this wa—!" The radio went dead.

La Flaga bent over the intercom. "Captain! Get your ship out of there! They've gained control of the port. We're on our way out." It was La Flaga's job to provide escort to the cadets stationed on the Archangel. Now he was going to show these newbies how things got done.

> > > > >

Outside, on the upper deck of the Morgenroete factory, a young, platinum blond Coordinator turned to his companions. "It's exactly like Commander Creuset said," he murmured. The cold tone of his voice matched his icy expression.

Yzak Joule was a first class ZAFT pilot—constantly in competition with Athrun. Athrun, for his part, kept as much distance from Yzak as he could.

Next to Yzak, Dearka Elsman snickered. "If we poke them, perhaps they'll come running out of their holes." With straw-colored hair and dark skin, the cynical, hot-blooded pilot made a good counter-balance for Yzak. Athrun got the distinct impression Yzak and Dearka made for a dangerous combination.

The team watched as things became confused and chaotic down on the Morgenroete factory floor. Their ZAFT battleships must have been detected and caused a panic. They watched as the chestnut-haired female officer in a factory uniform gave orders. She motioned to a trailer loaded with huge containers.

"That's the one," Athrun said. "Our target."

Yzak smiled. "Naturals really are stupid, aren't they?" He pushed the transmitter button.

Athrun squatted beside Nicol Amalfi, fifteen years old, (only one year younger than himself, but infinitely more fragile-looking) whose gentle features and quiet manner belied his incredible talents as a pilot. Athrun noticed his nervous gaze. He tapped Nicol's arm and the kid gave him a little grin.

Behind them, Rusty McKenzie teasingly jabbed Nicol in the back. They were all teenage boys, but as Coordinators with heightened abilities, they performed their duties like adults. This mission was no exception.

"It's time," Athrun said.

The counters hit zero—explosions ripped through the factory district—people and equipment were blown apart in the inferno. Secondary explosions tore through the walls. Bedrock crumbled inside the mine. Debris fell like rain.

Mobile suits broke through the port and descended on Morgenroete. The killing machines gouged buildings with rifle fire and disintegrated passing vehicles. All hell broke loose. Countless blast tremors rocked the transport station as the new weapons convoy tried to navigate through the pandemonium.

Sensing the advantage, Athrun and his team moved in.

> > > > >

Kira and the stranger locked gazes. Without warning, a roar swept through the building, followed by a terrific shaking. The sound was deafening.

"What the—?!" Sai yelped.

"Did a meteorite hit us?" Kuzzey asked.

The students dashed out of the lab and made for the elevator. Kira nearly lost his footing as they scrambled over each other. The elevator shaft was destroyed so they headed for the emergency stairs.

A factory worker ran up the stairwell.

"What happened?" Sai called.

"We're being attacked by ZAFT!" the worker yelled.

"Mobile suits are in the colony!"

"What?!" the students shouted.

Kira stood stock-still, shocked. The factory worker motioned them to follow as they hurried through the building.

The newcomer suddenly changed directions and went down a corridor.

"Hey! You!" Kira shouted. Without thinking, he spun on his heel and ran after the stranger.

"Kira!" Tolle called.

"I'll be right back!" Kira yelled over his shoulder. He tailed the boy all the way to the factory area before catching up.

He grabbed hold of the slender arm—when an explosion knocked them off their feet. The boy's hat blew off, revealing a very feminine face. Kira stared down into those golden eyes, bewildered.

"You're a . . . you're a *girl!*"

The stranger glared daggers at him. "Well, what the hell did you think I was?"

He could feel her trembling. She had such a cold, unapproachable way of carrying herself in the lab; he'd just assumed she was a very skinny boy. Now, looking at her . . .

An awkward silence settled between them, broken only by a series of distant explosions. Eventually the girl shook free of Kira's grip and stood.

"Why are you following me anyway? Just go away!"

"Go away where?" Kira challenged, getting to his feet. "We can't go back to the labs." The corridor had collapsed in the blast.

Kira thought quickly and grabbed her hand. "I know! This way!" He took off running.

"Let go of me!" she demanded. "Idiot."

"Idiot?" he muttered, tugging her harder so she would keep up. He looked back, startled to see tears in her eyes. Kira stopped, loosening his hold on her.

"There's . . . there's something I must see!" she said. "It's already too late, isn't it?" She looked down, talking to herself. "I thought this would happen."

"You *what?*" he asked, frowning. How could she have predicted a ZAFT attack? Was she psychic or something? There wasn't time for this! The place was falling down around them! "Tell me later. We've got to evacuate. If we can make it to the factory quarters, maybe we can still get to a shelter."

He interlaced their fingers and ran.

> > > > >

Outside the factory, a fierce battle raged. The Earth Alliance Force sent out mobile trailers loaded with surface-to-air missiles, but the GINN (standard, streamlined ZAFT mobile suits) rushed in and crushed the armored vehicles like toys. The Earth Forces had been caught completely unaware.

Athrun's team infiltrated the factory and headed directly to the transport exit. Three trailers that carried the Earth Force's new weapons were right ahead of them. Strapped down on those trucks were none other than Earth Alliance's first group of mobile suits!

ZAFT marksmen expertly took out the Earth Force soldiers guarding the suits. Yzak swiftly leapt atop the rear trailer and ordered, "Destroy anything you can't steal! There should be five mobile suits. Are the other two still inside?"

Taking the lead, Athrun said, "Rusty and I'll go check it out! You secure these three!" He signaled to Rusty to head toward the transport exit.

"I'll leave it to you, then," Yzak agreed. He turned to Dearka and Nicol, who were already climbing into the Earth Force mobile suits. "When you board them," Yzak warned, "make sure you disable their self-destruct mechanisms immediately!"

> > > > >

Kira and the girl jogged along an upper passage that opened to a large hangar bay. Before them stretched a thin catwalk, several feet above the factory floor. Kira could see the emergency shelter far ahead. He grabbed the girl close and set out.

Below, a gun battle erupted between the ZAFT Army and the Earth Force soldiers who were dressed in factory uniforms. But what were Earth Alliance Forces doing on a neutral colony?

Explosions caused the catwalk to sway. Kira barely managed to get the girl safely to the other side. What he saw then rooted him to the spot.

"Whoa," he breathed.

A huge mobile suit sat on the floor ahead of them. It was amazing, regal and severe, gleaming like a statue of some pagan god. Kira had never actually seen a mobile suit outside of pictures in textbooks and on video games. It had reflective steel armor and four sharp horns sprouting out of its head. Staggeringly complex, it was clearly different from its ZAFT counterparts.

The girl banged her fists on the walkway's railing. "The Earth Alliance's new suit! So it *is* here!" She dropped to her knees, shoulders shaking, grasping the railing until her knuckles turned white. "Father!" she shrieked. "You traitor!"

The word *traitor* ricocheted off the factory walls.

Kira saw a flash out of the corner of his eye. He tore the girl from the railing just as bullets spat against the wall and grazed the catwalk. Dragging her listless body for several feet, Kira used all his strength to reach the entrance of the emergency shelter.

He pressed the intercom and a voice cracked through the speaker, "Is someone still out there?"

"Yes!" Kira answered. "It's me and I've got a friend. Please—open up!"

"Two of you?" the voice worried.

"Yes!" Kira said, ducking another barrage of bullets.

Seconds ticked by, each one an eternity. "We're already maxed out here," the voice said. "Shelter 37 is down the block on the left! Can you make it there?"

Kira turned and looked. It wasn't far, but to get there they'd have to go straight into the crossfire. He could do it—alone. "Just take one of us! Please! She's just a girl!"

A pause before the shelter door unlocked, its light flipping from red to green. "Okay, we'll let just her in. Sorry!"

The door whooshed open and Kira pushed the girl inside the chute. She broke out of her stupor and frowned. "What are you doing?"

"I'm going to the next shelter," he responded quickly. "I'll be okay."

She reached out for him, but he punched the lock and the glass door slammed shut. He watched her lips form the words *wait* as she was whisked down into the underground shelter. He checked the lock; she would be safe.

He turned, heading back toward the factory.

Kira could make out a woman's voice below. "Hamana! Brian! Hurry! Move out the X105 and X303!" He looked down through the catwalk's grate and saw her: chestnut hair, factory worker uniform, and a mean-looking rifle in her hands—standing on top of the mobile suit's fuselage. She was taking heavy fire.

Kira spotted a ZAFT sniper taking aim at the woman. Before he could think about his own safety, he warned, "Behind you!"

She reacted immediately, spinning around to nail the sniper right in the eye. Returning fire, she called to him over her shoulder, "Get over here, kid!"

"It's okay! I'm going to the shelter one block over!"

Firing her rifle, she hollered, "It's totally gone. There's nothing left but a door! We're moving out!"

Smoke billowed above the block to the left. Kira's gut instincts told him to trust this woman. He made a swift decision, catapulting from the catwalk and dropping more than fifteen feet to the factory floor. With seamless agility, he landed next to her like a cat atop the mobile suit.

The woman blinked at him.

Across the way, her teammate protected the mobile suit alone. He let loose his rifle and bulls-eyed a ZAFT soldier.

"Rusty!" a young voice called out.

A red-suited pilot leapt out into the open, firing at the rifleman who had taken Rusty's life. The bullets found their mark—the Earth Force soldier crumpled to the ground.

"Hamana!" the woman screamed.

The red-suited pilot spun around and fired at her, hitting her in the shoulder.

"Gaww!" She dropped her rifle as she fell against the mobile suit, blood spurting where hot metal had met flesh.

The enemy took aim, got her in sights, and fired . . . Click: ammo empty. He dropped his gun and drew out a long blade. Stalking over to the mobile suit, he climbed atop and raised his knife high.

Kira abandoned all reason, operating purely on instinct, and threw himself between the woman and the pilot, crouching low.

The enemy soldier paused. ". . . Kira?!"

Startled, Kira looked up. The soldier's helmet was smeared with blood; flames reflected in the visor. He squinted until he could make out the face . . . the eyes.

I'm sure we'll meet again.

"Ath-Athrun?"

The pilot visibly trembled at the name. Kira could see his reflection in those haunted green eyes. The two of them faced each other, speechless.

Taking advantage of the pause, the woman whipped her gun up. Athrun jumped out of range just as the bullets burst forth. Kira turned and tackled her with a growl, tumbling them both into the cockpit of the mobile suit. She winced in agony.

Athrun approached a second time, knife gripped firmly in his hand. The woman punched a console button and the hatch to the cockpit slammed shut.

"Get behind the seat," she ordered. Clearly she was no pilot, but she understood the suit's command systems. "If I could just move it . . ."

Kira slid in the back as gauges lit up and the mechanized motion of the engines rapidly increased. A monitor switched on; they could see outside. Kira could just make out Athrun's red pilot suit as the boy dashed toward the second mobile suit.

Athrun . . . a ZAFT soldier . . . it was insane. Athrun hated war. Athrun promised him it would never come to this. It couldn't have been Athrun. And yet—

Kira's thoughts were broken when strange letters appeared on the monitor:

General
Unilateral
Neuro-link
Dispersive
Autonomic
Maneuver

Kira looked at the shiny red letters. "Gun . . . dam?"

Life breathed into the mobile suit—its eyes shown on. The engines keened. Its huge limbs jerked. The bolts securing

the fuselage to the maintenance bed fell away. With stiff movements like those of a toddler, the mobile suit rose up amid flames and took its first steps.

> > > > >

In space, just above Heliopolis, ZAFT mobile suits battled against Earth Force mobile armors. Mu La Flaga piloted his own Moebius Zero, closing in on a ZAFT GINN. His gun barrels deployed, surrounding his red fuselage. He tracked his target with perfect aim.

No one else in the Earth Force could handle those gun barrels; La Flaga was truly special in that he could strike at dead-angles and shoot at multiple targets simultaneously. Once, at the Grimaldi Front on the Endymion Crater of the moon's surface, he managed to single-handedly shoot down five GINNs. (The standard Moebius had less than a fifth of the strength of one GINN; hence, it took a five-to-one ratio of force for the Earth Alliance to keep up with a ZAFT offensive. It was the equivalent of La Flaga taking down twenty-five Moebiuses.)

Since that day, he'd been nicknamed the Hawk of Endymion.

A GINN hit the escort plane to his side; it dive-bombed into the mine section of the colony's asteroid. A fireball ensued. La Flaga squeezed the trigger and pierced the shoulder of the GINN, breaking its arm off.

He caught sight of several strange mobile suits leaving the spaceport. "What the hell?" he mumbled.

The three Earth Force mobile suits, known as the X Numbers or the G Weapons, slowly approached the ZAFT battleship. These new models had been developed in top secrecy—but just that quickly they had been stolen! There must have been a leak. A spy for ZAFT.

La Flaga bit the inside of his cheek and raced forward.

> > > > >

"The Aurora's been shot down! Emergency retreat!"

On the bridge of the Vesalius, Commander Creuset raised an eyebrow.

Captain Ades could hardly fathom it. "The Aurora? Damaged? In this little fight?"

Even ZAFT's most basic pilots were superior fighters and this outfit was composed of the crème de la crème. How could they possibly be defeated by the small military operations of a neutral colony?

Commander Creuset stared out into space and then suddenly laughed. He had spotted the Zero. "It seems there's a fly in need of a good swatting."

"Sir?" Captain Ades asked.

Creuset squared his shoulders and announced, "I'm going out there."

> > > > >

Deep inside Morgenroete's mining shaft, Natarle slowly regained consciousness. A huge explosion had jettisoned her up against a wall, knocking her out.

Thin smoke clouded the hangar. Debris—and corpses—floated in zero gravity. She remembered hearing about the ZAFT invasion . . . receiving orders from the captain . . . running from the command booth amid alarms and confusion.

Then there was the explosion and sudden darkness. Now there was only silence.

"The Archangel," she gasped. She had to protect it. Kicking off the wall, she floated in zero gravity toward the command booth. It had been completely destroyed—the front glass panels were shattered; faint emergency lights cast an eerie glow. The dock outside was a total disaster area: cranes toppled over, the catwalk was in pieces, even the Archangel teetered at a bizarre angle.

Natarle glanced back at the captain's lifeless body as it floated behind her. She felt like the strength had been zapped from her limbs.

"Ensign Badgiruel?"

Startled, Natarle spun around. Chief Petty Officer Neumann peeked over a passageway. "Neumann!" she exclaimed, grateful she was not the only survivor.

Before she could ask, he said, "Only a few people on the ship made it out unharmed. Just about all the factory workers are gone." He led the way to the Archangel. They entered the ship from an unhinged hatch.

The survivors gathered on the deck. Natarle wondered at how few of them there were. There were no other officers except her and she was a mere ensign lieutenant.

She headed straight for the bridge. Natarle went to the pilot's seat and flipped switch after switch. She breathed a sigh of relief as the lights, consoles, and screens started up without a hitch. "That's our Archangel. She wouldn't sink so easily."

Neumann looked worried. "The debris is too dense around the harbor entrance. We're completely sealed in."

Natarle nodded and opened a communications channel. Ear-splitting noise shot out of the intercom speakers; the electric wave interference was still going strong.

That gave her pause. If the Archangel had been the target of the attack, then their ship would already be crawling with ZAFT soldiers. But after the initial explosions—nothing. However, the electronic wave interference meant the hostilities continued. So were they simply out to attack the industrial colony, or . . .?

She jerked forward. "The ZAFT. They're not after the Archangel." Frowning, she whispered. "They're here for the Gundams."

> > > > >

Loudspeakers continually reported the following message through the deserted streets: "Heliopolis is officially under evacuation order Level Eight. Citizens should proceed to the nearest evacuation shelter immediately."

Athrun powered up his stolen mobile suit and rocketed away from the surface. The face of his childhood friend, fighting back tears as they parted, flashed through his mind. He shook his head, but the image remained.

"No, it wasn't him," he whispered allowed.

Kira was supposed to be on the moon, not in the middle of Heliopolis. How could he possibly have anything to do with the G Weapons?

The pilot of the GINN who had destroyed the last remains of the production factory, Miguel Aiman, appeared on Athrun's monitor. "Well done, Athrun!" he said.

Did Kira make it out in time?

Athrun bitterly replied, "Rusty's dead. There's an Earth Force officer piloting the machine we left behind."

"What?" Miguel choked. "Rusty?"

Athrun bit his lip and nodded. Rusty had been the most cheerful pilot among them—the only optimist in their little group. When things got rough, Rusty buoyed their spirits and encouraged them to stick together. Now the very glue that held them together was gone.

Miguel's face twisted with rage. "You go on. I'm going back for that damned machine."

> > > > >

Murrue struggled to land the Gundam in the city. Its feet touched the ground but it still titled dangerously. Kira clung to the back of her seat to keep from falling over. Despite her injury, Murrue frantically adjusted levers and throttles, but the suit's movements remained awkward, as if it had been lamed.

On the monitor, shots of Heliopolis changed every few moments, each image worse than the previous one. Kira looked at them, aghast. Tree-line streets, grassy parks, rows of shops—decimated into mere hunks and piles of burning debris and ash.

In the corner of the screen he could see people running through the streets. He leaned forward, astonished. "Sai? Tolle? Miriallia!" he exclaimed. Couldn't they find an evacuation shelter?

A gray GINN appeared in front of them, firing its machine gun with three inch rounds. The bullets dug craters under their feet. The Gundam lurched off balance, flinging Kira over the seat.

"Wah!" His head burrowed into the woman's ample chest.

"Get back!" she yelled. "Do you *want* to die?"

"S-sorry," Kira stammered, blushing. He moved over. The GINN filled every inch of their monitor as it brandished its saber. Kira screamed.

The woman pushed a button on the control panel and suddenly the mobile suit's reflective steel armor shone bright blue. Its limbs went ivory white. The GINN's saber swung down over their heads and Kira closed his eyes—CRASH!

A groaning sound, scrapping metal: their Gundam had grabbed the GINN's saber between its shining white hands.

"What the—?" Kira gulped.

"The GINN's saber won't work against the Strike," the woman said.

"The Strike?"

"That's the suit's name. I've activated its Phase Shift System. The steady electrical current strengthens the body against gunfire and missiles, as well as enemy swords." Now the Strike's armor glowed a bright blue, with deep crimson burning down its chest and stomach.

The GINN pressed in again. The woman squeezed the trigger and the Strike's head-mounted vulcan sprayed bullets, but missed. The enemy used that opportunity to kick out, sending the Strike a reeling blow. They stumbled back, nearly demolishing a building. The GINN charged, bringing its saber down onto the cockpit again and again.

The woman held her breath, frantically working the controls. Kira watched helplessly. Outside, Tolle and the others scrambled to hide in the debris as the two giant machines battled. Tolle grabbed Miriallia out of harm's way as the Strike's feet stumbled to and fro.

Kira saw their plight and snapped. He pushed the woman's hands away, grabbed at the controls, and pulled a lever. The Strike's body ducked then thrust forward to attack.

On the ground, Tolle and his friends watched, wide-eyed, as the Strike shoved the massive GINN back.

Kira turned to the female officer and said, "There are people down there, you know! If you're gonna pilot this thing you have to be careful!"

She grimaced. "Why you little—"

But Kira was already fiddling with the computer gauges. "What a mess," he griped. "How can anybody move a machine with such a crude operating system?"

"It's not finished," she replied defensively. "The new OS hasn't even been installed yet!"

"Aw, look, just . . . just get out of my way, please," he said. The fallen GINN started getting up. "Hurry!" he barked at her.

She slid over and Kira jumped into the seat. Pulling out the programming keyboard, he started typing with terrific speed. With one eye on the screen's windows and the other on the GINN, he instinctively calculated the moment of the next attack and weighed it against their system's immediate needs.

"Reset the Zero Moment Point and CPG while calibrating," he murmured, typing away. "All right. Connect the control module directly to the pseudo-cortex's molecular ion pump!" Mumbling to himself, clucking his tongue and cursing a bit, Kira furiously rewrote the Gundam's operating system.

The GINN's saber swiped in. Kira was ready. He manipulated the triggers and levers with one hand and typed with the other. The Strike's vulcan spit out rounds and this time hit their mark—the GINN's sword arm was blown back. He checked his work. "Neural linkage network reconstructed, meta-motion parameters revised, feed forward control restarted, transmission functioning. Motion routine connected. Systems online! Bootstrap starting up!"

Kira saw the GINN heft its machine gun, so he pressed down on one of his pedals. The Gundam instantly responded, jumping high in the air. The GINN leapt after it. Kira was sure to keep an eye on the people and buildings below as he called up the specs.

"Okay . . . What are our other weapons? Armor Schneider?" A blueprint appeared on the monitor. Besides the vulcan mounted on its head, he also had assault knives that were stored at the hips. They flashed on and off. "Is that all this thing can do?" he cried.

He pushed a button at random and the huge knives sprang out. Grasping them, he soared toward the GINN. The ZAFT suit answered with wild bursts of its machine guns.

Kira's eyes widened. "Not on *my* turf, pal." He weaved through the line of fire and closed in on the GINN.

"St-t-top!" the woman screamed as the two titans barreled toward each other. Kira thrust the sharp edge of the Armor Schneider into the GINN's neck joint. Its electrical system spouted flames. The GINN froze, lost its balance, and fell sideways.

The woman stared at the monitor in astonishment. Then she turned her wide eyes on him. Kira had never seen anyone look at him with reverence before.

"I'm Lieutenant Commander Murrue Ramius. *Who* are *you?*"

> > > > >

"This is Miguel Aiman! Emergency! I've lost control of my machine!"

As Miguel's panicked voice came over the cockpit intercom, Commander Creuset frowned. No one expected resistance like this. First, damage to the Aurora and now Miguel had been defeated. This meant the mobile suit they had failed to steal was infinitely more powerful than they'd imagined.

Creuset readied to leave in his personal mobile suit, the CGUE—the next generation of GINN. This machine had a bulked up, pearl-gray body and could move at astounding speed. Over the suit's intercom, he ordered Captain Ades on the bridge, "When I sortie, recall all the mobile suits. Give the enemy a taste of Equipment D."

"E-equipment D?" Ades stuttered. It was their heaviest weaponry, used for capturing fortresses in full-scale battles. Creuset laughed at Ades' puzzlement and started up his CGUE.

The commander spotted La Flaga's Moebius Zero as it returned to Heliopolis. He approached the colony slowly, his nerves jangling. "Just as I sense you, you sense me too, huh? The call of revenge links us . . . Mu La Flaga." His voice dripped with pure hatred, and at the same time, a strange kind of joy.

His CGUE closed in.

La Flaga, whose sharp eyes and sharper intuition had no doubt picked up Creuset's presence, dodged gunfire and slipped behind the CGUE easily. His red gun barrels deployed, firing at Creuset from all four angles.

Creuset evaded, hissing, "You're always, always standing in my way, La Flaga! Perhaps I can return the favor?" He feigned attack and suddenly changed course. "Inside Heliopolis we go," he murmured.

He could practically hear La Flaga cursing his name—for certain the Hawk of Endymion knew whom he faced. They could recognize each other's signature styles as easily as looking in a mirror. There was a cold sort of fear, a shudder up the spine like a hot blade, whenever they fought each other.

> > > > >

La Flaga followed the ZAFT suit as it zipped down and through the main spaceport. In a flash, Creuset was inside Heliopolis, heading into the Central Shaft, toward the zero gravity of the factory district. The CGUE weaved between factory buildings, using them as shields, turning occasionally to fire back on the Zero. It was a cowardly move.

He tried to align his sights, but he couldn't fire on Creuset without damaging the shaft. Pressing the advantage, Creuset fired rounds and took out his gun barrels one by one. La Flaga gritted his teeth in frustration, narrowly dodging the CGUE as it turned on him like a wild animal.

Then, the CGUE's rifle turned on the Central Shaft's wall.

"No!" La Flaga gasped, horrified.

Creuset fired, blowing a hole through the shaft, slipping inside the colony.

"Dammit!" La Flaga cursed, diving after him. He flew out to the surface, his eyes shifting to where black smoke bellowed. The Strike's glowing suit stood high above the vanquished GINN.

"The last machine," La Flaga whispered.

Creuset must have seen it as well; the CGUE flew straight toward the only remaining X Number. La Flaga desperately tried to intervene. "No. You're not getting this one," he growled.

The two machines buzzed around each other, trading volleys as if locked in a bizarre ballet. A heavy gauge bullet pierced the Zero's fuselage.

"Uugh!" La Flaga winced as his mobile armor flailed back. Out of options, the Zero retreated, a tail of black smoke trailing after it. All he could do was watch, helpless, as the CGUE swooped down on the X Number.

> > > > >

Aboard the Archangel, Neumann strenuously protested, "Launch the ship? With this tiny crew? Impossible!"

Natarle didn't pause from her startup preparations. She gave him a withering look. "Morgenroete is still under attack! Are you suggesting we simply sit here? Why don't I just grab you some chips and you can watch from the commissary in style?"

Petty Officer Tonomura came back with more personnel. "As ordered, I've brought all the crew who can help."

Natarle raked the new staff with her gaze. "Take your seats. Do as the computer instructs you."

Neumann persisted. "If there's still a ZAFT ship out there, there's no way we can fight!"

"I know that," she said coldly. "But there's no choice. We'll prepare to fire the special guns. You can still do that, can't you, *Officer* Neumann?"

Shamed, Neumann took his seat and grabbed the intercom. "Start launch sequence. Omit C30 and L21. Main motive power, online!"

Behind him, Tonomura reported from his console, "Output rising, all systems normal. Four hundred fifty seconds until nominal."

"Too long," Natarle complained. "What's the state of the Heliopolis energy conduit?"

Tonomura checked his readings and replied in surprise, "It's . . . active!"

"Hook in our power from there."

"Conduit, online," he said. "Connecting to the accumulator." The launch sequence rapidly progressed. "Output power: contact. Engines normal! All systems online!"

Neumann looked over at Natarle. "Launch preparations complete!"

Her voice rang out, "Seal the bulkheads! All personnel, brace for impact! I want maximum battle speed when we fire the main guns . . . Archangel, launch!"

> > > > >

BOOM! A sonic blast shook Kira in the pilot's seat. A CGUE closed in from above!

Murrue gasped at the sight of the specialized GINN. "Get back," she strained, clasping her wounded shoulder. "Get back to Morgenroete! We can't fight a CGUE with these weapons and we've used up most of the batteries. We need additional power or the Phase Shift Armor won't work."

Bullets pounded their fuselage. Kira hollered as Creuset continuously fired. The Strike lost balance and fell, knocking Murrue unconscious.

"Ugh!" Kira feverishly pulled at the levers, trying to stand, but the CGUE readied a deathblow.

ROAR!

The bedrock collapsed around them as the huge, shimmering Archangel surfaced like a whale lurching out of the ocean.

Kira stared. "A battleship? Inside the colony?"

The Archangel blotted out the sky. Kira was dazzled by its scale and peculiar appearance. Multiple missiles shot from the ship's stern, hurling toward the CGUE. The ZAFT suit retreated down the Central Shaft, releasing decoy fire to stop the missiles. One missile broke through the decoys and followed the CGUE, striking the main shaft.

The ground shook.

Creak! Creeeeeak!

"No way," Kira said. He dove into the Morgenroete building and spotted the trailer. "Hey! Are these weapons?"

Silence. Murrue was out cold. He needed to get her medical attention—soon.

Biting his lip, he operated his Gundam's arms to open the trailer and pick up the Launcher Strike Power Pack. He adjusted it on the Strike's back, added another vulcan, and picked up a long barrel gun.

Calling up the data on his monitor, Kira read the weapons information quickly. He pulled out an alignment scope and waited until the ZAFT suit was in his crosshairs. Then he pulled the trigger.

Kira's field of vision went momentarily white. A massive blast of energy shot out as a thick beam of light, tore off the CGUE's arm, and then punched through the colony's outer wall.

"Ahhh!" Kira screamed, agonized. Heliopolis!

The colony's shell grew white-hot and curled outward. A huge, gaping hole remained. Kira paled.

"Wh-what kind of power is this?" he murmured.

He never thought a single mobile suit could do so much damage. It was beyond excessive. It was insane. The will to fight sapped out of him. He shut down, his expression blank, as the enemy suit escaped through the newly formed hole.

> > > > >

Athrun made his way back to the Vesalius with the stolen X Number, haunted by Kira's face. He had always believed he would one day be reunited with his best friend, but never like this. Though he tried to deny it, in his heart, he knew it was Kira. No mistaking that expression—those dark eyes.

Below, he saw the white-hot laser beam punch through the colony wall and shoot out into space. The atmosphere was sucked out, its water vapor instantly freezing into a misty snow. Objects caught in an outward flow sparkled in the sunlight, like dust filtering in a bright room.

Commander Creuset bit out over the intercom, "I have been shot. All units retreat."

Shot? Impossible. If the commander got shot . . . Athrun knew it was his duty to return the stolen mobile suit to ZAFT. But in the back of his mind, Kira's image burned. He had to know.

Athrun steered his machine back to Heliopolis.

> > > > >

"Amazing! How does it move?"

"Gundam? What's a Gundam?"

"Never mind that, she needs first aid, you guys. Ah, she's waking up!"

Voices drifted in and out. Murrue slowly regained consciousness. She realized she had been placed on a park bench. A black-haired boy peered anxiously into her face.

Sitting up, she was surprised to see the Strike kneeling off to the side. Several kids were climbing in and out of the cockpit. Murrue brandished her pistol and aimed it at the boy's extended hand. His eyes widened. "Who are you?"

"Kira Yamato."

She turned the gun onto the civilians in the mobile suit. "Get away from that machine!" she bellowed. A painful jolt ran through her aching shoulder. The kids blinked at her. She fired a shot over their heads.

"What do you think you're doing?!" the boy shouted.

Murrue pointed the pistol straight at his nose. The children finally came down from the cockpit. "This is the army's most highly classified secret. It's not to be tampered with. Especially by civilians."

The children screwed up their faces at her. She sighed. These school kids couldn't possibly grasp the situation. Besides, the one she was really angry with was herself—in a moment of weakness, she'd blacked out, and lost sight of Earth's most precious weapon.

Her eyes rested on Kira. The ability he'd shown piloting the Strike was almost *inhuman*. A whisper of a doubt ran through her mind . . .

"As I said, I'm Murrue Ramius. I'm a Lieutenant with the Earth Alliance Force. You have seen our top secret weapon, so, you'll all have to come with me until I make a report and figure out what to do with you."

The kids did not take this well.

"Go where? Why?"

"What about our parents?"

"We don't have anything to do with the army, lady!"

"We're citizens of Heliopolis; we're neutral!"

Her patience wore thin. She fired another round into the sky. "Enough!" She glared at them. "Do you really think that you still belong to a neutral state? That the war has nothing to do with you? Look around you!"

The Central Shaft had already begun making automatic repairs, but the hole in the outer wall could not be fixed. They could all glimpse the stars twinkling out in space. "This is war. Like it or not, you're now a part of it."

> > > > >

Natarle ran down the Archangel's ramp and called out, "Lieutenant Ramius! You're all right!"

Murrue steered the trailer loaded with Strike parts—and the students—toward the battleship. "I'm glad to see you. And the Archangel," Murrue responded. "You really saved us out there."

A handsome blond man sauntered up, grinning. "So sorry to interrupt this little reunion." He straightened up slightly. "Lieutenant Mu La Flaga, of the Seventh Mobile Fleet. Very pleased to meet you." He wagged his eyebrows at Murrue.

"Ah. Uh, Murrue Ramius, Earth Force Zone 2, Fifth Special Division," she responded, amazed to meet the Hawk of Endymion in person.

The three of them automatically saluted and then La Flaga turned to Natarle. "Requesting permission to board. My ship was destroyed by the ZAFT. Who's in charge of the Archangel?"

Natarle looked down, carefully composing her features. "All other commanding officers were killed in the attack.

Therefore, I think Lieutenant Ramius should assume the captain's post."

"Huh?" Murrue said, frozen stiff. Captain? Of the Archangel?

La Flaga shrugged. "I was escorting the new recruits to the X Number mobile suits. Any chance they . . . ?" His question hung in the air. Finally, Natarle shook her head and La Flaga's handsome smile tightened. Anger flashed in his eyes.

Before he could respond, a petty officer jogged out to them. "Ensign Badgiruel! You're needed on the bridge immediately!"

"What's wrong?" she asked.

The young officer turned to the ace pilot. "There's another mobile suit coming in fast!"

"Hey," La Flaga said, "You're talking to the wrong person, kid. *This* is your new captain." He patted Murrue's rigid back. "Time to get in the driver's seat, huh?" he whispered to her.

"M-me?" she stammered. "What about the Strike? It's still outside!"

"No time to retrieve it," Natarle insisted, running back to the ship. "It can join us on its own. Prepare to launch!"

The ship's alarm sounded. Murrue glanced over, looking inside the trailer, and saw Tolle hug Miriallia close. "I hope Kira will be all right."

BOOM!

They looked up to see the hole in the outer wall expand, and then a hoard of GINNs zoomed through in tight formation. Murrue made her way to the bridge, fast on La Flaga's heels. The GINNs were on the monitors, each one equipped with missile launchers and long barrel particle guns.

La Flaga shot her a wry smile. "Aw, man. They're using heavy demolition equipment to attack this little base? Talk about overkill. Think they're feeling a little inadequate?"

Murrue blinked.

Behind the GINN formation, one of the Earth Force's mobile suits glowed a deep red. Tonomura looked at his readings and gasped. "It's the X303. The Aegis!" Gloomy silence descended over the bridge: their own weapon would be used against them.

Murrue clenched her fists. "So, this is how the Aegis will fight its first battle." She looked at the crew—they were afraid. They were untested. Only the Hawk had any real battle experience.

Taking his cue, La Flaga said defiantly, "All right. So that machine is now working for the enemy! But most of you know it like the back of your own hands. You really gonna let it sink you?"

Natarle commanded, "Prepare the Corinthos canon to fire; use laser guidance!"

"Solid projectiles won't work against Phase Shift," Murrue said. "Link the main gun radar and use scattered focal points!

Take care not to damage the colony, but our first priority has to be to escape Heliopolis!"

> > > > >

Even though Kira wasn't a soldier, Murrue had ordered him to remain in the Strike and he'd obeyed. Kira rummaged through the equipment outside the factory, looking for additional weapons, but his attention snapped back to the monitors when the explosions heralded the GINN invasion.

If they used those long barrel guns inside the already weakened colony . . . He picked up the large container labeled Schwert Gewehr—Sword Striker—and opened it. Inside was a sword almost fifty feet tall, strong enough to tear through a battleship's armor. Looking up at the hole he'd created in the colony's wall, he worried that this new sword might prove just as fatal.

He raced the Strike forward and leapt high. The lock-on warning blared in the cockpit—a GINN had fired a missile at him! He instinctively switched to evasive maneuvers. The missile doggedly pursued him all over the city, then suddenly looped around and blew into an axial shaft.

The connection between the ground and the Center Shaft ripped apart like cheap paper, causing the axial shaft to jut violently into the air. It crashed down, crushing several buildings into powder.

Kira screamed in frustration. The colony could not survive this kind of abuse.

Two more missiles launched. Kira glared, clueless as to how he could save the colony but still defend himself. The missiles raced towards him . . . closer . . . closer . . .

He flew out to meet them head on. The mobile suit closed in on the missiles—a terrific explosion roared! Its blast engulfed everything in fire and smoke.

The Strike leapt out of the rising smoke. Kira had taken a hit to the shoulder with one missile, but he'd managed to cut the other missile in half with his Schwert Gewehr. Narrowing his eyes at his enemy, he brought his sword down, screaming, "Ahhh!" One blow sliced a GINN's trunk in two, its fuselage instantly exploding. Panting, Kira looked up to see the red Aegis flying overhead. It was the same mobile suit he'd seen Athrun steal from the factory floor.

Athrun . . . Kira shook his head. Athrun wouldn't do this.

Over the radio intercom, he heard his friend's voice: "Kira? Kira Yamato?"

Kira choked back surprise. "Athrun Zala?"

"Oh, Kira . . . it is you, after all." Athrun sounded so sad.

The battle raged all around them. Missiles launched from the GINNs, mercilessly pounding the Archangel. The battleship couldn't fight back in full force without damaging the colony. The GINNs easily evaded the Archangel's missiles, leaving the weapons to detonate inside Heliopolis.

The Archangel launched another volley—it struck a GINN in midair, but its propulsion gas sparked and the GINN exploded into a fireball that set a nearby axial shaft ablaze. The inferno dismembered the shaft; it landed with a thunderous groan.

Kira watched, aghast, as missile after missile slammed into the ground. "Why!" he screamed at Athrun. Tears welled up but did not fall. "*How* could you do this? To a neutral colony!"

The Central Shaft creaked forebodingly, its body shuddering as it began to collapse.

WHOOSH—CRAAAACK!

The colony's backbone gave way, remaining axial shafts snapping like matchsticks, one after the other—SNAP SNAP SNAP—striking the ground at an accelerating pace. The Central Shaft's frame twisted, warping and whining in agony. The colony's outer wall shook under the weight of its own spinning centrifugal force and the entire structure of Heliopolis began to crack. Fissures ran through the outer shell like little bolts of lightning.

"What about *you?*" Athrun cried. "What the hell are you doing aboard that thing? You're a *Coordinator*, Kira! Why are you piloting an Earth Force Gundam?"

The controlled atmosphere got sucked up in a jet stream through the holes in the outer shell—whole chunks of buildings and various pieces of debris flowed up like paper getting sucked into a fan. Familiar houses, shops, and elecars were torn asunder by the vacuum. Roofs blew off. Glass shattered. Roads were pulled apart. The gape of the holes increased. Explosions ballooned, then vanished as they were sucked out into space.

"Heliopolis . . ." Kira whispered, horrified.

Cracks spread all around his Gundam. Flying debris continuously tackled his fuselage. The assault was relentless.

Below, the emergency shelters ejected as lifeboats, flinging out among loose elecars and spinning rubble. The colony split wide open.

The force yanked Kira's Strike up; he lost all control. He tried to fire his propulsion engines, but they simply spun him directly into the outgoing jet stream.

"Ahhhh!"

"Kira!" Athrun called out, stretching the Aegis' arms to try and grab hold of his friend, but the distance between them was too great.

The Strike, along with the scattered colony, was swept out into space.

> > > > >

"X105, Strike, come in. Come in. Come in, Strike. Do you copy?" The radio intercom in the cockpit droned on steadily, desperate to make contact, while the Strike floated aimlessly in space.

Kira sat there, gripping the handles, breathing in and out sporadically. Heliopolis had been totally destroyed. Nothing remained. Why?

Chunks of the colony floated past the Gundam: a battered vending machine, a road sign, trees with the roots drizzling soil into the emptiness. Life was precarious—Kira got the message loud and clear.

"X105, Strike! Can you hear me? Kira Yamato, come in!" Murrue called.

He snapped out of his trance at the sound of his name.

"Kira, if you hear me, please, please respond!"

Kira switched on the intercom. "Yeah."

Her voice shot back, the relief unmistakable, "Are you all right?"

"Yeah."

"Can you locate your position? Can you make it back to us?"

He adjusted levers and set his course for the battleship. "Yeah. I think so." As he worked the machine, the control panel blurted out a strange electronic message. A blip appeared on the radar.

"A rescue beacon?" he wondered aloud.

A cylindrical-shaped object floated ahead. Kira tuned his radio to the beacon's frequency. "Hello? Anybody out there?"

An immediate response: "Yes! Our propulsion system is broken! We're drifting!"

Kira adjusted course toward the floating pod. He started thinking about his parents—how many people had made it out? All he could do was pray.

> > > > >

The Archangel's hatch opened and the Strike entered the arrival deck, cradling a rescue pod in its massive hands. Murrue grimaced. On the one hand, Kira had returned the Strike unharmed. But on the other, a civilian lifeboat meant nothing but trouble.

Murrue activated the bridge's intercom and began reprimanding him for it. Kira did not take it like a soldier. He, in fact, took it like a sixteen-year-old boy, which should not have shocked Murrue, since that's exactly what he was. "So you're telling me I should have ignored it?" he grumbled over the intercom. "There are innocent civilians inside."

Standard protocol insisted that during battle, lifeboats were responsible for themselves until a rescue cruiser could pick them up. Kira had no way of knowing that. She sighed. "Fine. I'll allow it—just this once."

A subordinate officer spoke up, "We're not supposed to pick up refugees in the thick of battle."

Murrue pinned him with her stare. "They can't help being totally stranded. I don't have time to argue with you, either. Close the hatch."

> > > > >

The huge airlock shut tight. The Strike entered the main hangar, where a battered mobile armor sat, horribly damaged, to the side. Kira's hatch opened and he peered outside.

The crew instantly started murmuring and whispering about him.

When he'd heard the news, Maintenance Officer Murdoch had come straight from the showers, a towel still wrapped around his neck. He ran a hand over his stubbled chin and gruffly said, "So, a kid was piloting that thing?"

Kira's friends came running into the hangar, rushing up to him. They took turns hugging and jumping on him, slapping him on his back—he'd never felt so popular.

"Hey, yo, Kira!" Tolle exclaimed.

"Thank goodness you're okay!" Miriallia cried.

Sai ruffled his dark hair. Kira rolled his eyes, laughing.

A girl's voice rang out from the doorway, "Sai!" Red hair trailing behind her, Flay ran out from the crowd of refugees in the pod. She leapt into Sai's arms.

Surprised, but clearly pleased, Sai slowly wrapped her up in a hug. She buried her face in his shoulder and cried, "What's going on? What happened to Heliopolis? I got separated from my friends and I was so scared, Sai!"

Kira's expression darkened a bit at their sudden intimacy. But . . . everyone was all right. That was the most important thing. The rejoicing students didn't notice as La Flaga walked right up to Kira.

"Well, well. I *am* impressed," he said.

Kira involuntarily drew back as the tall soldier invaded his personal space.

La Flaga smiled. He swept Kira with his eyes. "You're a Coordinator, aren't you?"

The words hung there in heavy silence. Everyone stared at him. Heat crept up Kira's neck. He squared his shoulders.

"Yes."

The crew raised their guns and aimed dead center at his chest.

His parents were Naturals. But they had him artificially created with enhanced abilities. Originally, Coordinators were designed only to have a stronger immune system, as a countermeasure against various epidemics that had broken out on Earth. But as the Coordinators' modifications spontaneously surpassed all expectations, fear and prejudice spread and an intergalactic boycott against their race began. Coordinators were in exile. And Kira? Kira was caught in the crosshairs. Heliopolis had been his home and both his friends and family were Naturals. But even *he* couldn't deny his Coordinator capabilities.

Tolle jumped in front of the guns and put his arms out wide. "What are you doing?" Kira's eyes bugged out as his friend flew into a rage. "He's a Coordinator, okay, but he isn't your enemy! He just fought ZAFT to save us all! Weren't you watching?"

The guns now turned on Tolle.

"Put. Those. Weapons. Down," Murrue ordered, her voice brooking no argument. Reluctantly, the Earth Force soldiers obeyed. "Heliopolis was a neutral nation's colony. There were Coordinators living there who didn't want to get mixed up in this war."

"My parents are Naturals," Kira felt the need to explain. "I'm first generation."

"Well, hey," La Flaga said warmly, "I'm sorry to have caused such a ruckus." He lightly tapped Kira on the shoulder. "I was just curious. I've watched a lot of good cadets work hard at becoming Strike pilots. In all our simulations, they could barely get the thing moving." He smiled gently at Kira. "You're quite a pro, kid."

> > > > >

Murrue, Natarle, and La Flaga gathered on the bridge, watching the monitors. Murrue nodded to the officer manning the observation station. "Can you detect the movements of any ZAFT vessels?"

Petty Officer Pal looked at his screens. "No use. There are so many objects in all that wreckage. Everything's giving off heat after the explosions . . . it's impossible to tell with radar or infrared."

"Well, at least ZAFT is in the same boat," La Flaga said. "They can't see us either."

It was a small consolation. Murrue murmured, "If we're attacked now, we won't stand a chance."

"You got that right, sister," La Flaga replied. "We only have the Strike and my hunk of junk Zero. It would be the shortest battle ever." He sighed. "This ship is pretty fast, right? What if we hit maximum speed? Out run 'em?"

"They've got a high speed Nazca-class." Murrue shook her head. "I don't know if we could make it."

La Flaga eyed her. "So, what's left?" This haughty pilot was testing her. "Surrender?"

Murrue narrowed her eyes into slits. Yes, she'd been thrust into the captain's chair without any real battle experience and, yes, she was probably way out of her depths. She could sense the crew's diminishing faith. But she was no coward.

"Surrender is not an option. We cannot hand over this ship—or the Strike—to ZAFT. No matter what, we must return safely to Atlantic Federation Headquarters." Though how they would ever make it all the way to Alaska now . . .

The Hawk of Endymion nodded but said, "What are we going to do if we can't make contact with the moon base? I appreciate your enthusiasm, but that won't shield us." So, he wasn't just pushing her boundaries. He was truly at a loss.

Natarle suddenly brightened. "Captain, what about stopping off at the Port of Artemis?" Murrue and La Flaga broke eye contact to look at her. "From this position, it's the closest course to any friendlies."

"The Umbrella of Artemis, eh?" La Flaga murmured.

The Archangel was property of the North Atlantic Federation. Artemis, a satellite colony, acted as a military base for the Eurasian Army, which was an ally. They were relatively close and would perhaps offer aid.

La Flaga wasn't exactly optimistic. "Neither the Strike nor this ship have been announced to the public. We're so new, we don't even have friendly force recognition codes."

"But even if we took a straight course to the moon base, you don't think we could possibly avoid a fight, do you?" Natarle countered. "And we launched without taking any supplies . . . we're going to need those *badly*, very soon."

Murrue frowned. The decision was hers to make. "I think we can get Eurasia to see our side of things. Given the present circumstances, we need to avoid confrontation with ZAFT as much as possible. We'll restock on Artemis, and then make contact with the moon base."

La Flaga looked at her, raising an eyebrow. "So, Artemis it is."

At La Flaga's suggestion, Murrue sent out a decoy ship to throw ZAFT off their trail. Then she ordered the Archangel to switch to inertia navigation, keeping the engines as quiet as possible and using the thrusters sparingly to avoid detection.

The Hawk of Endymion gave her a little half-smile. "A silent-run to Artemis will take about two hours." He watched as the crew worked frantically. "Let's hope our luck holds."

> > > > >

Captain Ades stared out of the large window panel on the bridge of the Vesalius. A slight tremor coursed through him and, try as he might, he couldn't stop shaking. "If only I'd known this would happen," he lamented.

Fear gripped him. He turned to Creuset, who looked cool and confident. "What are we going to do? We've destroyed a neutral nation's colony. The Supreme Council will never forgive us."

Creuset didn't so much as twitch. "How can you call a colony neutral when it built the Earth Alliance Force's latest weapons?" His entire demeanor was placid, calm. "Most of the civilians escaped. This incident is nothing compared to the Bloody Valentine."

Certainly not. There'd never been anything to equal the scale of that massacre. Women and children . . .

Creuset suddenly frowned. "Ades. Can't you locate the enemy ship?"

The captain fought to hide his surprise. "You mean to keep after them? We've already lost two mobile suits, yours notwithstanding."

"But we have four more, don't we?" Creuset's voice was as soft as a bolt of silk.

"The stolen X Numbers? You want to send those in?" Ades blinked.

"As long as we can finish extracting their data in time, it makes no difference to me." Creuset fixed him with a look. "We cannot let that ship get away."

A communications officer spoke up, "I've picked up a large heat signature. Could be a battleship. Based on its coordinates, it appears to be headed for the Earth Force's moon base."

Creuset paused, raising an eyebrow. "No." He shook his head. "It's a decoy. I'm certain of it." He raised a strategic panel and brought up a map of space.

Ades stared at the man. He would never understand the way Creuset's mind worked.

"We'll cast a net," Creuset whispered.

"A net, sir?"

"The Vesalius will fly on ahead of them and wait." Creuset's finger traced a straight line to the Port of Artemis. "The Gamow will take this course and follow them at a distance." His finger made another arc across the map. "The Naturals' battleship will have nowhere to go."

Ades frowned. "Artemis? But, sir . . . what if they really *have* gone to the moon?"

Creuset straightened. "It's too far for them to go. I sense they are headed for the Artemis base. Summon the Gamow. We're launching the Vesalius."

Captain Ades couldn't find the logic in it, but he obeyed his orders nonetheless.

> > > > >

La Flaga, star pilot, frantically waved his hands in front of him like a frightened schoolgirl. It was kind of endearing, but mostly just annoying. He sat in his living quarters, leaning as far away from Murrue and Natarle as possible.

"But we may need the Strike's power," Murrue insisted, "and you're our only pilot, Lieutenant."

"Are you *kidding?*" he choked. "Have you taken a gander at the OS data that kid rewrote? Do you think I, or any normal person, could really use something that complicated?"

Murrue thought back to when Kira had revised the Gundam's operating system. He'd worked at lightning speed and under attack, no less. His skills were confounding. In truth, the minute he touched it, the Strike was like a new machine altogether.

Natarle offered, "We'll just put it back the way he had it before. We can't entrust the mobile suit to a civilian, much less to a *Coordinator.*"

Obviously Natarle had a deep-seated hatred for the Coordinators. To her, even the word *Coordinator* was a synonym for enemy. Most Naturals felt that way. Murrue thought that Coordinators were nothing more than special human beings—they didn't *ask* to be different—and yet, she could sympathize with her fellow Naturals.

La Flaga sighed heavily. "So, what? You want me to go out there and become a very pretty target?"

Murrue and Natarle shared a look. It seemed out of character for the Hawk of Endymion to downplay his fighting abilities, but he had a point.

"Listen, ladies," he said, "the boy's got a lot more to him than mere technical knowledge. He's not just an engineering protégé; he's got excellent mechanical instincts. He's got them in spades. A pilot who can manage programming—and still have that kind of maneuverability—well, let's just say, without him your new toy would be worthless."

> > > > >

At the other end of the living quarters, the students huddled together in a room. Still shocked by the obliteration of Heliopolis, and uneasy about the prospect of brand new battles, the mood was pretty heavy.

Kira lay on the bed, totally zonked out.

Flay watched him sleep, her expression both disgusted and awed. "So, he's a Coordinator?" she whispered.

Sai replied, "I'm amazed he can sleep, given the current situation."

"He's completely worn out," Miriallia said. "He had a really hard time out there."

Kuzzey chuckled. "A hard time? The things he did out there . . . they're not hard at all for a . . . for someone like Kira."

"Whatcha getting at, Kuzzey?" Tolle pressed.

"Nothing. But they said Kira rewrote that Gundam's OS. Now, when do you think he had the time to do that? During the fight, that's when."

Everyone but Flay had seen Kira fight. The Strike had transformed with Kira at the helm. Tolle and Miriallia had always known that Kira was a Coordinator; he'd made no attempt to hide the fact. That was why Professor Kato always had Kira work on the hardest lab assignments. But no one imagined his overwhelming skill with a mobile suit.

Kuzzey continued, "Coordinators find all that stuff easy. And everyone in ZAFT is like that. *Everyone.*" He glanced over at Kira, curled up on the bed. "Do you think the Earth Force stands a chance?"

The group cast timid glances at Kira's sleeping face. He looked innocent, like any normal teen. He looked just like one of them. Up until this moment, no one had thought of Kira as anything other than an incredibly smart friend. A little timid. Quirky. Aloof. But genuinely likable.

Now, the gap between them seemed infinite.

"Yo, Kira Yamato!" La Flaga called from the doorway.

Tolle nudged Kira awake. The boy blinked sleepily. "Mm?"

La Flaga jerked his head toward the door. "We need a moment alone. Pilot to pilot." The students quickly filed out of the room and shut the door.

They stood outside awkwardly. A few moments passed, and then Kira's voice burst out from behind the door, "I won't do it!"

> > > > >

La Flaga watched the boy's gentle features harden. The kid was afraid. He stood rigidly, wide-awake, hands clenched at his sides. The top of his head didn't even reach La Flaga's shoulder.

"Why do I have to get in that thing again?" He crossed his arms. "Maybe you're right; maybe we are part of this war now. But we didn't choose it. My family moved to Heliopolis *because* we don't want anything to do with it! Please don't involve me again!"

La Flaga looked at the boy silently for quite some time. He took a deep breath. "Kid. We've got no other choice. You're the only one who can pilot that thing."

"I'm not a soldier."

Grimacing, La Flaga got right up in the boy's face. "So, when the next battle goes down, you'll die—and let your *friends* die—because you're too scared to go in again?"

Kira fell silent. His features went slack. La Flaga had his number now: Kira was a hero at heart. "You and I are the only ones who can protect this ship."

"But, I . . ." the boy's voice wavered. La Flaga saw the conflict deep within and he couldn't help feeling for Kira.

He put his hand on the boy's shoulder. "Hey. You have a singular ability. You know you're special, right?" he said quietly. "Trust that. It will see you through."

Kira looked up at him, agonized. La Flaga was startled to see such emotion. The boy dropped his head bitterly, pushed the older man aside, and ran from the room.

> > > > >

Le Creuset sat behind his desk. His office was dark and cold. He lifted his eyes when Athrun suddenly came in, saluted sharply, and announced, "Athrun Zala, reporting as ordered, sir!"

The commander motioned Athrun to be at ease. "I've been putting off talking with you," he said quietly. "I suppose you know why I've brought you here."

"Yes, sir. For blatantly ignoring an order, sir." Athrun's back was ramrod straight. "I'm very sorry."

Creuset nodded. "I've no intention of punishing you. I just wanted to hear what you have to say for yourself." He leaned forward. "That wasn't like you, Athrun."

Athrun ducked his head. Creuset slowly stood up and walked over to him, caressing his shoulder. "Without accurate information from subordinates, a commander can make mistakes in planning, right, Athrun?"

"I-I'm sorry. I was upset. It was . . . unexpected. That last machine, the one we failed to capture—it was piloted by a boy named Kira Yamato. He was a grade school friend, back on the moon. I never would've imagined seeing him on the battlefield." Athrun paused, composing himself. "I went back to make sure it was him. He's also a Coordinator, you see."

Creuset listened eagerly, his head cocked to the side. "Tsk. War is full of little ironies, isn't it?" He sat back down and steepled his fingers. "No wonder you were so upset. Were you good friends?"

"The best."

"Ah. I understand." Creuset paused. "That being the case, I'm excusing you from the next excursion."

Athrun looked up in surprise.

Creuset explained, "You'd have to put a gun to your friend's temple. I won't make you do that, Athrun."

The boy shook his head. "No, Commander. He's being used by the Naturals. Even though he's superior to them in every way, he's too nice, too easygoing. He doesn't know what he's getting into!" Athrun planted his palms on Creuset's desk and leaned forward. "I want to try and persuade him to our cause, Commander. He's a Coordinator. He'll listen to me."

Creuset sat very still. "I understand your feelings, dear boy, but what if you're wrong? What if he *doesn't* listen?"

Athrun took a breath. "Then," he looked Creuset right in the eye, "I'll shoot him down."

Creuset smiled.

> > > > >

Alarms blared. The Archangel's bridge was in chaos. Officer Pal shouted, "Large heat source detected! One hundred and twenty five miles, Mark 3317 Yellow, Charlie." He paused. "It looks like a battleship's engine!"

Natarle looked up from her instruments. "It's right on our tail. The exact same course. They couldn't have spotted us yet, could they?"

Officer Pal said, "The ship is moving at high speed on an horizontal axis. It's a Nazca-class."

La Flaga stared out into space for a moment. "He's read our minds. They're going to try and outdistance us and then meet us head on."

Murrue frowned at him. "How can you be sure?"

He met her eyes. "I'm sure."

She took the captain's chair and nodded to Officer Pal. "What about the Laurasia-class?"

Pal hurriedly checked his readings. "There is a heat source advancing at one hundred and eighty-six miles from behind. Starboard side."

They were caught between the two ships.

Silence filled the bridge for several tense moments.

La Flaga spoke up, "The Nazca-class will see us soon. It will definitely pursue. If we use our engines to retreat, the Laurasia-class will be right up on us." No way out. The Hawk of Endymion frowned, thinking. "Hey," he said to Pal, "display the data for both battleships. Put a space map here."

Murrue looked at him blankly. "You've got a plan?"

He sighed at her and muttered, "That's what we're going to do right now."

> > > > >

The intercom announced: "Enemy ship spotted! All crew report to your posts immediately!"

Miriallia and the others looked up. "Is the ship going into battle?" she asked.

Soldiers scrambled out of their rooms. The crew had barely had a chance to rest, but now they were pulling on uniforms and dashing to their designated positions.

The intercom came on again: "Kira Yamato to the bridge! Yamato to bridge!"

"I wonder what he's gonna do?" Kuzzey asked.

Sai mumbled, "If he doesn't fight, I think we're all in real trouble."

The students looked down. "Tolle," Miriallia pulled on his sleeve, "are we just going to sit here and wait for Kira to protect us?"

Tolle had been thinking the same thing. "You're absolutely right. There's gotta be some way we can help out. Who's in?" There were some tasks only a Coordinator could accomplish, but that didn't mean they'd have to burden Kira with everything. Tolle stood up and resolutely looked at each and every student. They nodded, one by one, and without a word, made their way to the bridge.

> > > > >

Kira heard the urgent announcement, but his feet felt like lead as he made his way to the bridge. The expectations on him during this crisis pressed in like a vice—tighter and tighter. If he refused to fight, the Archangel would most likely sink. His friends, the refugee civilians, the crew would all perish. He couldn't save them single-handedly, but without the Strike, they didn't really have a prayer.

He didn't want to fight. He didn't want to die. He didn't want to stain his hands. The ZAFT mobile suits had living, breathing pilots in them. He didn't want to kill them. Certainly, he didn't want to kill Athrun. He couldn't breathe.

Turning a corner, Kira stopped short. His classmates ran toward him, all dressed in Earth Alliance Force uniforms. An officer escorted them to the bridge.

"Tolle . . . Sai . . . ? What are you doing in uniforms?"

Kuzzey spoke up, "They said if we go on the bridge we have to be in these."

"The bridge?" Kira didn't get it.

"We thought we'd help out on deck," Tolle explained. "They're short-handed, right? Well, we're able to handle the computers and controls just as well as anyone else."

"ZAFT uniforms are cooler, though," Sai complained. "I feel like a costumed idiot; I don't even have an insignia."

"Ah, yeah," Tolle interrupted, "because of all our experience: none!"

Officer Chandra, who was escorting them, rolled his eyes. "Come on, then."

Kira stood there, dumbfounded. "You guys . . ."

Tolle grinned. "Hey, if you're gonna risk your neck to protect us, it's the least we can do. We've got your back, buddy."

Miriallia nodded enthusiastically. "We'll do our best! All of us!"

Kira was at a total loss for words. For the first time in his life, he was not alone.

> > > > >

La Flaga had secretly been hoping Kira would show up. A few minutes after the announcement, the kid popped into the hangar bay, his new pilot suit a little loose around his thin frame. The pilot looked the boy up and down. "Finally decided to put on a decent outfit, I see."

Kira looked him square in the eye. "Like you said, Lieutenant: we're the only ones who can defend this ship right now. I don't want to fight. But I *do* want to protect my friends."

La Flaga bristled. "Naturally. We all feel the same way, kid. No one here *wants* to fight. We do what we have to, to protect the ones we love."

That seemed to startle the kid. Did he think Naturals were trying to eliminate Coordinators on a whim? Out of pure hatred? Did he think they were warmongers? Ah, but those dark eyes were beginning to see—they were not so very different from each other, after all. Kira hung his head, clearly embarrassed.

"It's a little big for me," Kira said to change the subject, pulling at the neckline of his jumpsuit.

The Hawk of Endymion smiled. "You're a little small for a pilot, Skinny." He winked. Without wasting any more time, he brought Kira up to speed on their battle plan then accompanied the boy as far as the Strike and then headed over to his own Zero.

He felt Kira's eyes on him until his hatch closed. La Flaga climbed into the cockpit and brought up the operating system while tightening his seatbelt. His life—all their lives—now depended on that kid.

Murrue's voice came on the intercom, "Nazca-class behind us, at ninety."

La Flaga replied, "I've briefed Kira. We're all set. I'm moving out. Everything depends on timing," he told her. "I'll get the Nazca-class. You'll have to concentrate on the rest, Murrue."

"We will," she responded. "La Flaga . . . be careful out there." She swallowed nervously.

He smiled. No sweat. He had come up with the plan, after all. Once the enemy spotted the Archangel, they'd concentrate all their forces on it. It would give him the opportunity to sneak his Zero on the Nazca-class.

He radioed Kira. "All right, Skinny, you're on defense now. The only thing you should think about from here on out is protecting this ship. And yourself, of course."

"Yes," Kira replied. "You take care, too, Lieutenant!"

La Flaga laughed out loud. The newbie was worried for him. That was just adorable. "Mu La Flaga, departing from the Archangel. You guys just make sure I've got something left to come back to, okay?" He cut off communications and dropped the Zero from the ship's hatch. It fell straight down into space.

> > > > >

Kira watched La Flaga freefall and wondered if their plan would really work. The older man would move in on the enemy, but in order to get there, they would all have to buy him time. Kira had to defend the Archangel and he felt the weight of such a tremendous responsibility.

A familiar voice sprang over the intercom channel. "Hey there, Kira!"

"Miriallia?"

Her face popped up on the monitor. She looked . . . older . . . in her uniform. "From now on, I'll be relaying battle control commands for your mobile suit and the mobile armor. Nice to see you." She smiled and winked.

Behind her, Kira could see Officer Tonomura palming his face. "You're supposed to say, 'Do you copy?' "

Kira laughed.

Tonomura took over the microphone. "Your equipment this time will be the Aile Striker. The enemy will advance the instant you leave the Archangel. Do you copy?"

"Roger that!" Kira said enthusiastically.

A crane mounted the Aile Striker unit, made of wings and weapons, onto the back of his mobile suit. The wings were propelled by four vernier thrusters, which significantly increased his mobility in space. His weapons were sabers (one stored on each shoulder) and a two and a quarter inch beam rifle.

Kira checked the wings and then walked out onto the launch pad. Over the intercom, he heard Murrue: "Ready engines! On my signal, fire thrusters and the main gun simultaneously! Target the Nazca-class!"

The engines rumbled and the ship's gun powered up.

Natarle's voice boomed, "Now!" Blinding light gushed from the gun's muzzles and the ship's engines blasted on.

"Launch of Nazca-class' mobile suit confirmed," Officer Chandra said. "It's the Aegis."

Kira stiffened. Athrun . . .

Miriallia shouted, "Kira! Launch the Strike!"

"Roger." The hatch shot open. Kira's hands shook as he pulled the levers. He shut his eyes and thought of his Natural friends. "Kira Yamato!" he called out. "Gundam, departing!"

The launch pad catapulted the Strike, its battery cables stretching and then snapping off. Kira's face pulled back under the sudden G-force, which dissipated the moment he entered space's vacuum.

"Starting Phase Shift," Kira said. "Firearms' control lock released." The Strike's metallic gray armor turned into brilliant red, white, and blue as the Phase Shift shields went up. Then Kira searched the radar screen for any sign of the Aegis.

> > > > >

Murrue stood on the bridge, tense. Three heat sources were detected just off the stern; they had to be mobile suits.

"Load the missile launch tubes with heavy Corinthos!" Natarle ordered. "Start up valiant canons on both gunwales! Officer Pal, input target data as soon as possible."

Tolle and the other students focused on their work consoles as twelve missile ports opened for the huge canons.

"Ensign Badgiruel," Chandra called out, "it's the X Numbers: the X102, Duel, the X103, Buster, and the X207, Blitz."

Murrue froze. "They've thrown all our G Weapons into the fray. They think we won't destroy our own creations."

> > > > >

Kira heard about the three approaching Gundams on his radio. He ignited his vernier thrusters and hefted his beam rifle high as the Aegis approached, whizzing right past him.

Athrun hailed him, "Kira! Hold your fire! We're not your enemies!"

Kira *knew* it. He knew Athrun wouldn't try and kill him.

"You're a Coordinator too," Athrun continued. "You have no reason to fight us."

Kira thought back to Heliopolis, to the sight of the colony breaking apart.

"Why are you with the Earth Force, Kira? How could you side with those Naturals?"

Kira shot back, "I'm *not* with the Earth Force! But . . . but my friends are onboard that ship! I can't just let you—" Kira saw the two other mobile suits swoop in to attack the Archangel. This was no time for a chat. He steered the suit to intervene.

"Kira—stop!" Athrun shouted, cutting directly in front of him.

"Athrun," Kira growled impatiently. "Why are you in ZAFT? Didn't you always say you hated war?!"

A particle beam cut Athrun's answer short; it narrowly missed Kira. A voice shouted over the radio, "What do you think you're doing, Athrun?! What's wrong?"

Kira called up the mobile suit's data on his screen. "The X102 Duel . . . An X Number."

Of the five Earth Force mobile suits, the blue-and-white Duel had the most standard specs. Similar to the

Strike, it also had beam sabers on both shoulders, a beam hand rifle, and grenade launcher. And it was fast. Very fast.

The Duel chased after Kira, firing its rifle. "If this one's too much for you to handle, Athrun, then get going. I'll take it out!"

> > > > >

Two X Numbers, the Buster and the Blitz, viciously attacked the Archangel. The battleship was large and powerful, but up against such agile, deadly mobile suits; it was in a desperate battle for its life.

Murrue furiously shouted orders. "Fire anti-beam depth charges! Use the Igelstellung vulcan guns to keep those Gundams at bay! Fire Helldarts on automatic!" The depth charges shot out, scattered, and blanketed the ship in anti-beam particles. The vulcan gun towers on each gunwale automatically adjusted to track the mobile suits' every moment, while the anti-air missiles launched from behind the bridge.

The Buster returned fire with its high-energy convergent rifle. The anti-beam particles helped disperse the shot, but the beam was so strong, some of it managed to strike the ship's side. The Archangel rocked with impact, its white armor glowing an angry red.

The Blitz soared underneath the ship. The lower Igelstellung guns traced it and opened their muzzles. Murrue commanded, "Use the Gottfried guns! Roll starboard thirty degrees, then twenty to port!"

The ship rotated sharply, causing gravity to momentarily disappear in the living quarters. The civilians lost their footing and screams broke out. Flay clung to the bed frame as she was lifted off her feet.

The Gottfried discharged an array of heat beams but the Blitz managed to avoid them, barely. It became clear to Murrue that the Archangel and its young, inexperienced crew were surpassing the Coordinators' expectations, but still, they weren't out of the woods yet.

> > > > >

Kira could not shake the Duel. He wanted to help the Archangel, but his hands were full dodging the Duel's beam rifle. He took several hits to his armor and grunted.

So far, he'd been on defense, desperately trying to outrun the Duel. It wasn't working. He looked in the targeting scope, hoisted his beam rifle, took aim, and pulled the trigger, but the Duel nimbly dodged Kira's fire.

Frustrated and impatient to get back to the Archangel, Kira fired at random. Before he knew it, the Duel pressed in and brought down his saber. Kira shouted and just barely deflected the sword with his anti-beam shield. The two machines tangled together for a moment, rocking closer to the Archangel.

The Buster spotted them and broke away from the battleship. It activated its Phase Shift and the Buster's beige body changed to khaki and red. Taking its large missile launcher from its shoulder, the Buster aimed from the hip and fired right at the Strike.

Alarms blared in Kira's cockpit. With great difficulty, Kira swung out to avoid the missiles. Two against one—hardly fair. He couldn't tell up from down, he didn't know where to look, and he couldn't see what the enemy was doing. Frightened, he fired recklessly at anything that crossed his vision. Meanwhile, he took hit after hit to his armor. He didn't think to look at his energy gauge, but he was rapidly losing power and dropping into the red zone.

> > > > >

Onboard the Vesalius, a ZAFT officer announced, "Message from the Gamow! Enemy unit confirmed as the mobile suit Strike."

Creuset frowned. He *knew* that Mu La Flaga was onboard the Archangel; he could sense it. He knew that the Zero was damaged, but still operational. "The mobile armor hasn't come out yet," he muttered to himself. "Why?"

How could the Earth Force entrust their ship's defenses to this inexperienced fighter who spun around in a panicked frenzy, firing wildly? It didn't add up. He wanted to get out there, but his CGUE was still missing an arm . . .

"Approaching the enemy battleship! We will soon enter firing range."

Creuset nodded at Captain Ades. "Prepare to engage."

The captain protested, "But our mobile suits are still out there! They're right in the path of our main guns!"

He sighed and gave the man a cold smile. "Our boys won't let themselves get hit by friendly fire. Give them *some* credit, Ades."

Clearly Ades had something to say, but like a good little lapdog, he turned obediently to the crew and said, "Prepare to fire the main guns. Target the battleship."

> > > > >

The Archangel's bridge was a flurry of activity. Officer Chandra looked at his console and said, "I'm picking up laser exposure from the Nazca-class, Captain. They've locked onto us!"

Murrue paled. On their monitor, the Strike was barely fending off the enemy Gundams. What were they going to do?

Natarle rattled off orders without hesitation. "Prepare to fire the Lohengrins! Target that Nazca-class!" The Lohengrin guns were positron canons with enough power to bury a full-scale battleship with one direct hit.

Immediately, Murrue countered, "Belay that order! Lieutenant La Flaga is still approaching the enemy ship." If they fired with the Zero in the way, he would be decimated. She couldn't let that happen to him . . .

"If we don't fire now, we're finished," Natarle insisted.

Murrue remained steadfast. "My order remains not to shoot. All hands—evasive maneuvers!" Her clenched fists were slick with sweat. She knew they were critically outnumbered and inexperienced. If they strayed from La Flaga's plan, they were doomed. Should his surprise attack not succeed, they'd never make it to Artemis. She had to trust him.

> > > > >

Back on the Vesalius, Creuset raised his head from his schematics as if he'd heard someone call his name. The hair on the back of his neck stood up; it was that sixth sense of his, warning him of danger. He felt a strange mixture of hatred and joy, knowing that La Flaga was up to his old tricks.

"Ades! Full throttle the engines! Lower the bow. Pitch sixty degrees. Now!" he bellowed. Captain Ades stared at him as if he'd gone mad. Maybe he had, but that didn't make him wrong.

A control officer gasped. "Heat source approaching from below! It's a mobile armor!"

"Captain, *now!*" Creuset insisted.

> > > > >

The Hawk of Endymion let out a rebel yell as he soared at top speed toward the Vesalius. The battleship's thrusters suddenly roared on—but not in time. The Zero dodged the automatic defense systems. La Flaga deployed his gun barrels with lightning speed.

He blasted away at the battleship's engines, nonstop, using up his full arsenal. The target belched fire and smoke. "Aw yeeeah!" he shouted triumphantly.

Zipping up and over the Vesalius' helm, La Flaga shot grappling wires down to the ship's outer wall. Using inertia to swing back like a pendulum, he cut loose the wires and rocketed safely back out into space.

> > > > >

The bridge of the Vesalius shook violently. Klaxons blared. The ZAFT crew started talking over each other:

"Engine area badly damaged. Output dropping!"

"Fire! Seal bulkheads!"

"Enemy mobile armor is escaping!"

Ades watched the Zero zoom away, free and clear. "Shoot it down!"

Their battleship tilted drastically. They couldn't even align their sights, let alone lock on a target. That mobile armor had single-handedly moved the Vesalius into checkmate. Ades was shocked at the impudence of it all.

He looked over at Commander Creuset—he'd never seen the man so enraged.

"Damn you to hell, La Flaga!" Creuset roared, ripping the armrests off his chair and throwing them across the room. The half of his face showing beneath his mask twisted with hatred and fury. It almost looked like he was in pain.

Ades wisely remained silent; he'd never seen the commander lose his composer before.

> > > > >

"Receiving word from Lieutenant La Flaga: 'Operation was a success. Returning to the Archangel!' " Officer Tonomura said. Cheers filled the bridge. Tolle and the student refugees turned to each other and smiled, relieved.

Murrue loosened her fists, the knot in her stomach relaxing just a bit. La Flaga was okay. She quickly issued the next order, "Don't let it escape now. Prepare to fire on that Nazca-class!" Tension returned as the crew prepped the big guns. "Prepare to fire Lohengrins!"

The large gun muzzles opened. Natarle took her cue from Murrue and shouted, "Fire!"

The Lohengrins spat out whirls of plasma; they grazed the Vesalius' gunwales as the enemy ship scrambled to evade using wounded engines. A massive tremor rocked the Nazca-class—it was crippled and had no choice but to retreat.

> > > > >

Athrun couldn't bring himself to intervene in the fight between Kira and his ZAFT comrades. He'd not been able to break through the Archangel's defenses, either. So it was a failure all around. He gaped at the battleship's amazing display of firepower, wondering how the Vesalius was going to escape this one, when a laser communiqué from the Gamow came over the radio waves, ordering him to retreat.

The entire situation was in shambles. He watched a signal flare shoot up from the Vesalius. The X Numbers were being recalled.

Yzak, piloting the Duel, wouldn't let up, despite these orders. He rained fire down on the Strike obsessively. Poor Yzak didn't know that Kira was a Coordinator and *that* was why he could evade attacks so easily. Athrun knew the boy's pride was wounded, but still, it was his best friend out there.

"Yzak!" he admonished. "We've been ordered to retreat!"

But neither Yzak nor Dearka withdrew. Caught between the two X Numbers, the Strike couldn't approach the Archangel. Kira was trapped.

> > > > >

Onboard the bridge, Miriallia watched helplessly as Kira took heavy fire. Murrue leaned over her shoulder and hollered, "Cover him!"

Natarle interrupted, "What is this, a free-for-all?" A misplaced shot in close quarters would be deadly to both Kira and the Strike. And they had bigger problems. "Captain, I'm worried about the Strike's remaining power. It's been out there too long as it is."

> > > > >

La Flaga had been keeping an eye on the kid, watching the battle stats via laser communication the entire time. "Skinny can't come home, huh?" La Flaga shook his head. "Sheesh. Do I have to do everything around here?" he muttered as he rushed to Kira's rescue.

> > > > >

Kira gasped, his chest constricting. He couldn't hear the alarms over the sound of blood pounding in his ears. He pulled the rifle beam's trigger—no response. It was like a slap in the face. The gauges, the alarms—dead: he'd run out of power.

The color faded from the Strike's armor as the Phase Shift fell away. Of course, the Duel saw it and thrust ferociously with its sword. Kira froze—he was dead meat.

THUD!

Kira felt the G-force of sudden acceleration—his mobile suit was swept away! By the *Aegis'* taloned arm! Athrun had switched to mobile armor form, transforming into a transporter, grabbing the Strike in time to pull it out of harm's way.

"Kira!" Athrun called out.

"Athrun!"

> > > > >

On the bridge of the Archangel, Kira's friends all gasped. "The Strike's been captured by the Aegis. Its Phase Shift has fallen." Miriallia said.

A chill ran up Murrue's spine. This was her deepest fear—ZAFT now had all the X Numbers. And Kira . . .

"Kira! Kira! Answer me!" Miriallia screamed into the microphone. Murrue closed her eyes, wondering what she'd just done.

> > > > >

Kira sat in the cockpit, listening to the heated exchange on his radio. The ZAFT pilot of the Duel was chewing Athrun out.

"Athrun! What the heck are you *doing?!*"

"I'm capturing this machine, Yzak."

"Our orders are to crush it, you moron!"

Athrun huffed. "It's better to capture it! Now, retreat!" The Aegis rushed on, the other ZAFT suits close behind.

"Athrun! What are you planning to do?"

"I'm taking you to the Gamow," Athrun replied softly.

"No! Not to a ZAFT ship!"

"Don't be an idiot," Athrun gritted out. "If you want to live, you'll come with me. I don't want to have to shoot you, Kira."

"But Athrun, why are you doing this to me? Why ZAFT—?"

"My mother died in the Bloody Valentine. I . . . that's reason enough."

Kira fell silent. He was at a total loss for words. Mrs. Zala, dead . . .

A sideways blow struck the Aegis hard. La Flaga's familiar red Zero zoomed in front of Kira's monitor, its gun barrels deployed on all four sides. Athrun had to release the Strike in order to change out of mobile armor form and get back into mobile suit form.

La Flaga's deep voice filled Kira's cockpit, "The Archangel is gonna send you a Launcher Strike! Get out of there!"

"What?"

"Just turn on your navigation systems, kid. Get ready to exchange equipment!"

Kira looked back at the Aegis, now taking defensive position. "All right." He fled as the Aegis and the Zero charged one another.

He could still hear Athrun over the radio. "Kira! Wait—"
It tugged at his heart. He blasted the vernier engines, heading
for the Archangel.

The battleship laid down cover fire for him, but the Duel
stayed hot on his heels. The gap between the two mobile
suits lessened and Kira came close to panic. Suddenly, the
Archangel catapulted the Launcher Strike, as if pitching a
baseball, at Kira. He recognized the power pack and released
the Aile Striker from his back in order to make room for the
new weapon.

The target-lock alarm went off. The Duel had him in his
sights—it launched the grenades—the missiles sailed dead on
at the Strike.

BOOM!

> > > > >

Tolle, Miriallia, and Sai cried out as a huge explosion engulfed
the Strike. The Archangel fired a single beam that sliced through
the fireball, instantly hacking the Duel's right arm off.

Everyone stared in disbelief as the Strike sailed out of
the flames like a phoenix, its energized armor a bright red,
white, and blue. It had reached the power pack in time. A
whooping cheer rose up from the crew.

The Archangel spewed offensive fire at the Duel until
it had no choice but to retreat. They watched, giddy, as the

four X Numbers fled. Relief set in; people came down off the adrenaline rush. They had survived . . .

> > > > >

Vesalius' Pilots' Locker Room:

Yzak flung Athrun up against the row of lockers in the shower room. The blond's handsome face twisted in anger; he grasped Athrun by the collar. "You—how *dare* you? If you hadn't butted in like a glory-seeking idiot! Thanks to your blatant disregard of orders, the entire mission was a total failure!"

Dearka stood by, mumbling curses and egging Yzak on. Athrun remained silent and kept his arms slack. He and Yzak had never gotten along: Yzak held a long-standing grudge against him. Both Dearka and Yzak had strong ambitions and they regarded Athrun as their top rival. Athrun, in contrast, only wished to serve their cause and avenge his mother. He had no taste for uniform stripes and battlefield fame.

Yzak was about to lay into him again when the door opened. Young Nicol raised his voice, "What's going on here? Yzak, what the hell are you doing?"

"We had four machines, dammit!" Yzak spat back. "And we couldn't shoot down a single Natural! Not one, thanks to him!"

Nicol responded sharply, "The battle's over. It's done. No use blaming anyone now." Despite his quiet exterior, Athrun had always known that Nicol was a brave soul. With Rusty gone, the role of mediator would most likely fall to the younger boy.

Yzak glared at Athrun and then pushed him aside. He stomped out of the room, Dearka following close behind. With the two other pilots gone, Nicol relaxed his shoulders and came up to Athrun. "That wasn't like you, out there."

"Sorry." He shrugged, looking away. "I-I really need to be alone right now." Without another word, he walked out of the room and ran down the corridors. He pushed himself until he couldn't run anymore then he struck the wall with his balled fist.

He'd almost had Kira. They were so close. If only he could get Kira alone, reason with him, persuade him. But he'd lost the opportunity. The blood turned to ice in his veins when he remembered his promise to Commander Creuset: *I'll shoot him down.*

> > > > >

La Flaga flew his wrecked mobile armor into the Archangel's hangar, landing not too far from the Strike. The Gundam's hatch remained sealed shut, despite the fact that it had docked long before he landed.

He called out to Maintenance Officer Murdoch, "Hey? What's up with him?"

Murdoch shot him a look. "That boy," the maintenance officer swallowed, "he just won't come out."

Sighing, La Flaga climbed onto the mobile suit, punched the outer lock, and forced open the hatch. "Uuugh!" he grunted with effort.

Inside, Kira sat frozen stiff, his hands still gripping the levers. La Flaga pushed his way into the cockpit and crouched down next to the boy. "Hey there, Kira," he said softly. "Are you hurt? What's going on?"

Kira didn't even acknowledge his presence.

"Kira. Yo, Kira Yamato, snap out of it!"

The kid began shaking. His thin frame wracked and shivered. As if waking from a nightmare, he gasped for air.

The elder pilot couldn't explain the sudden jolt of pity he felt for this kid. Kira was just a teenager, an amateur engineer with no real flight training or battle experience. In the wake of the kid's extraordinary abilities, they'd all forgotten he was still just a kid.

Then again, it wasn't uncommon for new recruits to come back from their first battle vomiting, dripping with sweat, reeking of fear—only to go back out again full of confidence, having survived the initial ordeal. It would be the same with Kira, La Flaga sensed.

One by one, he eased Kira's fingers off the levers. Squeezing those small hands for a minute, he playfully used Kira's knuckles to knock on the boy's helmet. "Well done, Skinny." He pulled the visor off.

Kira blinked, still staring out into space with a haunted expression. The Hawk of Endymion looked into those big, dark eyes. "It's over, kid."

Kira relaxed a bit, still shuddering. La Flaga gave him a fatherly smile and shook his shoulder. "Neither of us got hurt. The ship is safe. You did good, my friend." He patted Kira on the back—this little Coordinator was certainly no superhuman.

Genetically superior or not, Kira was just a boy, teetering on the threshold of becoming a man.

> > > > >

The Vesalius, forced to stop pursuing the Archangel, took refuge by anchoring in the shadow of space debris. A communications officer handed a printout of a communiqué to Commander Creuset. The blond Coordinator glanced at it before handing it off to Captain Ades.

Ades scowled. "Even though we've come all this way, the Supreme Council summons us." As the PLANTs' supreme decision-making power, the council's requests were not open to debate.

"They are probably utterly confused about the destruction of Heliopolis," Creuset mused. "There's nothing we can do about that, at the moment." He chuckled.

This nonchalant attitude flustered Ades. "With the Vesalius in her current state, at the moment, we can't do anything at *all*. How go the repairs?"

Creuset cocked his head. "Nothing will hinder our purpose for very long. I want Athrun brought back from the Gamow. As soon as the repairs are finished, this ship will return to the homeland and the Gamow will continue to pursue that Earth Force ship."

Leaving the bridge, Creuset frowned, deep in thought. The council would ask them specifically to account for Heliopolis, he knew. He remained cool and indifferent, detached. Such matters were of little significance to the big picture. Even his prior fury with La Flaga abated somewhat. Now, he wanted that battleship.

> > > > >

The Archangel entered the Port of Artemis. Constructed on a remote asteroid in Space Zone 5, Artemis was a small, backwater Eurasian military base, famous for one thing only: it had an impenetrable defense shield known as the Umbrella of Artemis.

A belt of pure light wave energy, the device acted as the ultimate defensive shield. No object or weapon, not even lasers, could penetrate it. Murrue had to wonder, however, why a strategically insignificant base like Artemis even *had* such defensive technology.

The Archangel faced a serious dilemma. Constructed in extreme secrecy, the ship didn't even have military recognition clearance codes. Murrue wasn't sure they'd be granted access, but Eurasia seemed eager to welcome them.

As they approached the asteroid, La Flaga and Murrue traded a look. He made it a point to whisper in Kira's ear, "Lock down the Strike's startup program. Make sure no one but you can operate that Gundam."

They docked and immediately a phalanx of armed soldiers and mobile armors surrounded the Archangel. Without a word, the crewmembers were escorted to the ship's mess hall. "What is the meaning of this!" Murrue shouted. They motioned for her to sit at a table.

An Eurasian officer smiled at her. "We are simply locking the ship's weapons' systems and controls as a precaution. Your ship does not have any registered entry, so naturally we don't have clearance codes for it. We allowed you into the harbor after evaluating your situation, but we still haven't recognized this ship as friend or foe."

Murrue was shocked. If Artemis had truly thought there was even a *possibility* that they were enemies, the Archangel would never have been allowed into the port in the first place.

Armed soldiers led her, Natarle, and La Flaga to the Commander's Room. The man waiting for them introduced himself as Gerard Garcia, the base's commander. He was thick, short, and bald, but polite enough. "Welcome to Artemis," he said. "Whom do I have pleasure of hosting?"

Murrue, Natarle, and La Flaga introduced themselves. Garcia peered at them and then glanced as his computer. "Well, your IDs certainly seem to be those of the Atlantic Federation."

La Flaga's mouth tightened. "So sorry to put you to any trouble," he said with a hint of sarcasm. "I didn't realize we'd be so hard to recognize."

"Ah, yes," Garcia responded. "I've heard *your* hallowed name, Hawk of Endymion. For such a renowned solider to show up on such an impressive battleship, and to our far-flung little base, well . . ."

"We're on a special assignment," La Flaga said quickly. "I'm sorry, but we're not at liberty to discuss our circumstances."

Garcia narrowed his eyes. "Naturally. Regardless, I think the information pertaining to your 'circumstances' might be of particular importance to this alliance. Wouldn't you agree?"

La Flaga's face fell.

Murrue, however, was determined to keep relations running smoothly. "We'll need supplies as soon as you've finished verifying our authenticity. We must proceed to the lunar base without delay. Also . . . you should know, Commander, that there's a chance ZAFT might pursue us."

"Oh? ZAFT?" He smiled. "You mean like the ZAFT ship here?" He clicked a remote and a wall monitor displayed the Laurasia-class Gamow anchored not far from Artemis.

Murrue gasped.

Garcia leaned back in his chair. "They've been there for quite some time, just outside the Umbrella. But don't worry, loitering around is the best they'll do." He grinned at their nervous expressions. "You realize, of course, for the moment, even if you refit, you won't be able to leave."

"They're following *us*," La Flaga insisted. "If we stay, they'll let loose on your base. You are all in danger."

Garcia threw his head back and gave a great belly laugh. "Danger? On Artemis? How ridiculous!" He snorted. "Even the ZAFT know about the invincibility of our satellite defenses. They'll turn tail soon enough, just like all the others, without so much as setting a foot down on our soil."

Murrue stared at the commander in disbelief. Eventually his merriment subsided and he spoke courteously, "After they go, we'll get in touch with the lunar base. Until then, please make yourselves at home. You must be tired. I'll have your rooms prepared."

La Flaga raised an eyebrow. "Is Artemis truly as safe as you say?"

The commander looked him in the eye. "Neither lasers nor projectiles can pass through the Umbrella. It's as safe as your mother's arms."

> > > > >

The Gamow's bridge overlooked Artemis. On board, Yzak, Dearka, and Nicol were in a briefing meeting with the Gamow's commander, Captain Zelman. He was a classic military icon: trimmed beard, crisp uniform, straight shoulders, and a confident manner of speech.

Although he was the captain, military rank among the Coordinators worked differently than in the Earth Alliance Force. There was no regimented hierarchy in the ZAFT Army. Posts such as Captain or Commander and so forth were broad-based. Each soldier had high intelligence clearance and they never blindly obeyed an order. They worked within a system, certainly, but they were expected to be strategists and independent thinkers on the battlefield. Coordinators valued independence and equality.

Nicol stared at a graph of Artemis on a strategy panel. "There's just no way to break through the Umbrella," he said. "Not even with lasers. It's a real mess."

Dearka folded his arms. "You think the Naturals won't attack us again? What do you suggest—just wait until they feel like coming out?"

"Be serious, you guys," Yzak said harshly. "Do you want to send a report back to Commander Creuset, whose ship is out there, wounded, on the front lines, and tell him that we couldn't do a thing to help him? That would be a damned shame."

Nicol spoke up, "Hey. The Umbrella is always open, isn't it?"

"No," Dearka responded. "It's only activated against immediate threats. Most of the time, it's off—gotta save energy. But even if we try and approach while the Umbrella is closed, we'll be spotted well before we're within firing range and it will just come up again."

Nicol looked thoughtful. "My machine," he said suddenly. "The Blitz. It might be able to get by without detection." Until now, the other pilots had ignored him, but they all turned their heads at that. Nicol smiled mischievously. "See, it has this cool feature, even better than Phase Shift."

> > > > >

Back on Artemis, the Archangel's crew and refugees had no idea what was going on. They huddled together in the mess hall, whispering:

"Why won't they explain anything?"

"Where's the captain?"

"What's going on?"

Kira sat with his friends in the Archangel's commissary. Sai turned to him and asked, "Isn't Eurasia our ally? Do you suppose they've had a falling out with the Atlantic Federation?"

Kira shrugged.

"That's not It," Officer Tonomura said. "We don't have clearance codes."

Murdoch growled. "I think that's probably the least of their concerns."

Officer Neumann nodded. "Something's fishy with the Eurasians."

The name Earth Alliance Force was misleading. In truth, the alliance was formed in CE 70 with one common goal: wipe out the ZAFT Army. But various nations each had their own federation —the Canadian, North American, and Central American countries made up the Atlantic Federation; the European nations, (except for Northern Europe) Russia, and parts of Asia comprised the Eurasian Federation; the Republic of East Asia, and various small islands made up the East Federation. Together, they formed the Earth Alliance, but they could hardly be called a cohesive unit.

The rest of Earth had been divided up into neutral nations, like Orb—a group of Pacific Islands that owned space colonies, such as Heliopolis—or ZAFT-occupied areas, like Northern Africa. It was all very, very complicated.

The Archangel and the Strike were the hottest weapons the Earth Alliance had; the trouble was, only the Atlantic Federation knew about it. Eurasia was an ally, of course, but they had their own ambitions, projects, and budgets. It became painfully obvious how anxious the Eurasians were to get their hands on the Atlantic Federation's technology, when armed guards burst into the mess hall.

Commander Garcia stepped forward. "I'm this satellite base's commander," he announced. "There is a mobile suit aboard this ship. Where is its pilot?"

Kira started to get to his feet, but Murdoch put a hand on his shoulder and pushed him back down. The older man kept Kira firmly in his seat.

Neumann spoke up snidely, "What are you asking *us* for? Didn't the captain want to tell you?" To switch Garcia's focus on him, Neumann stepped in front of Kira. "Just what do you want with the Strike, anyway?"

Garcia grimaced, offended. Then he suddenly burst out laughing. He walked right up into Neumann's space. "Nothing in particular. We're just so *honored* to have the opportunity to see it before its public debut. We've so very many questions we'd like to ask. So . . . who is the pilot?"

Kira's heart raced. Now he knew why La Flaga wanted him to lock the Strike down. The Eurasians had tried to take the Gundam and found it wouldn't move without him.

Murdoch cleared his throat. "If you have any questions, you should address them to Lieutenant La Flaga. He's our star pilot."

Garcia wagged his finger. "We were monitoring the battle as it happened. La Flaga was in the Zero. After all, he's the only man capable of operating the Zero's gun barrels, right?"

They were monitoring the battles? They saw, but did *nothing* to help?

131

Garcia scanned the faces of the officers, growing impatient. "I doubt the pilot's a female, but who knows? Even your captain is a woman." Everyone remained staunchly silent. "Children for crew members?" Garcia seethed. "What kind of ship is this, anyway?" He reached out and grabbed Miriallia by the arm, yanking her harshly out of her seat. She yelped. "Tell me, girl, who is the pilot?"

Kira shot to his feat. "Knock it off!" he shouted. "I am, dammit."

Garcia tossed Miriallia to the side. "Boy, I give you full marks for nerve. But that Gundam is not a toy. Quit lying!"

The commander lashed out to slap him, but Kira's Coordinator reflexes allowed him to dodge. He grabbed Garcia's arm, twisting up until it almost snapped. The soldiers watched, wide-eyed, as Kira tossed Garcia unceremoniously to the floor.

Kira stood over him, indignant. "Don't even try it."

Garcia's face reddened in humiliation. A flick of his wrist and the Eurasian soldiers surrounded Kira, pulling his arms back behind him.

Sai leapt out in front of Kira. "Please, stop! Stop this!"

Garcia punched Sai's cheek, hard, and he fell to the floor. Flay screamed, clinging to Sai. "Stop it! Stop it!" She pointed at Kira. "He *is* the pilot! *And* he's a Coordinator!"

Murdoch and the crew grimaced. Garcia looked dumbfounded. Everyone stared at Kira. The commander motioned the soldiers to march the boy out of the room.

Tolle stamped his foot at Flay. "Why did you say that?"

"Because it's the truth," she replied coldly.

He narrowed his eyes at her. "Don't you care about what could happen to him now?"

"Don't talk to me that way! This is an Alliance base, isn't it?" Flay blushed. "Why *shouldn't* we tell them who the pilot is? Have you forgotten who we're fighting to begin with?" Flay didn't look the least bit guilty about ratting out their friend. Tolle had to quash the urge to strangle her.

> > > > >

Kira stood in front of the Strike in the hangar bay as Garcia and his entourage swarmed around him. "You want me to take the lock off the OS?" he asked dryly.

Garcia grinned. "Of course, be my guest. I want you to do more than that. I want you to analyze this thing's construction and propose a weapon that would be effective against it."

"I'm just a civilian. I'm not a soldier or an engineer. I can't do things like that." Kira crossed his arms.

"But . . . you're a traitor Coordinator. Right?" Garcia pressed.

Kira reeled. "Traitor . . . ?"

Garcia looked down his nose at Kira. "I've no idea why, but you've decided to betray your brothers. A Coordinator that sides with the Earth Force is a precious ally. Tell me, would it make any difference to you if you fought for the Eurasia Federation?"

Kira didn't like what the man insinuated. "You're wrong. I'm not— "

"No need to worry," Garcia assured, all smiles. "Eurasia will treat you well."

Traitor. Kira had never in his life felt so self-conscious. He'd never really thought about choosing a side—the war was always some distant, complex thing—and now he was being forced to take a stand. Either way, he'd end up hurting someone he cared about. It felt like there were no such things as friends anymore. People fell into one of two categories: ally or enemy.

Kira climbed into the cockpit and typed away at the keyboard with uncanny speed. The Artemis technicians marveled as he unlocked the suit's operating system. Soldiers remained right outside the hatch, guns poised and ready, afraid of what the Coordinator in their midst might try.

Back at school, the day Kira had confessed to his friends that he was genetically engineered, they were surprised, but they didn't care. Sai just laughed and said, "It doesn't change the fact that you're our friend, right?"

They'd teased him, asked him to help with their homework, and maybe watched him a little more closely out of curiosity. But they accepted him. Tolle and Miriallia were very protective of him. Those memories were precious—

perhaps even more so than those happy days on the moon with Athrun.

Outside the cockpit, Garcia eagerly watched Kira's hands and smiled. He reminded Kira of a wolf, licking his lips. Kira felt like nothing more than a tool. At least when Professor Kato had asked him to do things, he'd felt respected and appreciated. Those days were over. The Earth Alliance would make him dance like a trained monkey.

Being a Coordinator was his destiny, and now, his curse.

> > > > >

In the Artemis control room, monitors showed the ZAFT Laurasia-class ship in retreat. An officer went over the report. "The recon shows no enemy presence within the neighboring area. It's all clear. Inform the commander. Retract the circumference light wave defense belt. Switch to Level Two."

> > > > >

The Gamow had retreated from the Port of Artemis, but it was still well within range to detect the collapse of the Umbrella's intense energy signature. Nicol had been waiting; he launched the Blitz from the ZAFT battleship.

Dearka shook his head as he watched from the deck. Yzak stood beside him. "The Earth Force put together quite a defense," he said. "But Nicol's Gundam will do the trick. Even if he is a little coward."

As the Blitz advanced, streams of gas blew out of its jets, engulfing the fuselage. The gaseous particles surrounded the mobile suit and it slowly began to disappear. Nicol watched his readings. The Mirage Colloid—a specialized stealth system that warped electromagnetic waves, including visible light and radar, by wrapping the fuselage with magnetic fields—enabled the Blitz to become completely invisible.

The asteroid's rocky wall covered the Artemis base. On the surface, along with airducts and antennas, reflectors that created the light wave defense belt stood tall. Nicol hefted the Trikeros (a combination beam rifle, beam saber, and lancer dart) and attached it to his shield. He took careful aim and fired out a single, lethal shot.

> > > > >

The Strike's OS booted up. Its eyes ignited. Suddenly there was a dull, rumbling sound and the ground quaked. Garcia's deputy called over the intercom, "Control room, what's that vibration?"

A confused voice answered, "We're not sure. There's no sign of anything in the vicinity."

Another tremor rocked them hard, and then the ground shook violently. Whatever it was, it was damned close. The control room officer screamed in utter astonishment, "The Umbrella's gone! It's totally gone!"

"What?!" Garcia roared. "Gone? That's ridiculous!"

"We're under attack, aren't we?" Kira asked over the speakers. "There's no time to argue." He grasped the Sword Striker and approached the launch pad. The gantry crane swung a power pack onto the Strike and soon he was ready to go.

Kira looked down at his hands. What was he doing? How could he possibly cut down a Coordinator—one of his own? Just to save these people, who looked at him and only saw a freak show. He was angry and bitter, and filled with an overwhelming sense of loneliness, as he rocketed out of the ship's hatch.

> > > > >

Throughout the base, personnel scrambled around in confusion. The explosions distracted the Eurasian soldiers guarding in the mess hall. Officer Neumann led the other crewmembers to revolt—there was a brief scuffle—and then the Artemis guards were down for the count. The crew headed straight for the bridge while the refugee civilians stayed in the commissary.

"Start the engines!" Neumann said.

"What about the officers?" Tonomura asked.

"If we stay here any longer, this ship won't make it." Neumann shook his head. "You know they'd want that to be our first priority."

They powered up the ship, when all of a sudden, Murrue, Natarle, and La Flaga ran on deck—they'd managed to escape in the chaos as well. Instead of a salute, the crew gave up a thunderous cheer.

La Flaga walked up to Sai and peered at his bruised cheek. "Nice shiner, kid!" He ruffled the young man's hair. "So . . . what's *up* with this space rock, anyway?"

Sai answered sourly, "Let's not stick around to find out."

Murrue raised her voice, "Archangel, launch!"

Outside, the Duel and the Buster joined the Blitz. Artemis launched a single Moebius in answer, but without the Umbrella, it was no use. The Blitz harpooned it full of lancer darts and the Moebius went down swiftly.

The Buster had already infiltrated the base. It reached the control room and launched a single explosive. A staggering blast—the aperture gate of the base blew off and chain reactions blossomed on the asteroid's surface. Artemis had fallen.

From out of the fireball, the Archangel surged, scorched, but safe.

The New Century colony looked like a shining golden hourglass, twirling in space. Around its slender center spun a structure called the yoke. Two pyramid-shaped cones revolved at opposite ends of the yoke, each cone constructed of mirrors poised to collect sunlight. Inside the bottom of the cones were residential quarters, where inhabitants that worked the colony's organic farms lived.

Stretched along the colony's outer wall were acres and acres of self-repairing glass. These panels reflected sunlight. Hundreds of them lined the entire colony, making New Century shine brilliantly against the pitch-black backdrop of space.

This was a PLANT—home to the Coordinators.

Creuset escorted Athrun out of the Vesalius. They headed into the military station where a shuttle waited. Inside was a single passenger. The middle-aged man had noticeably sharp features and wore an elegant, brown business suit. As they approached, Athrun saw the passenger's face and stopped.

Commander Creuset smiled at the seated man, unsurprised. "Your Excellency, Defense Chairman Zala." Creuset bowed his head. "It's an honor to have you accompany us."

The man gazed placidly at Athrun. "You may dispense with the formalities, Commander."

Athrun brushed back his bangs. "It's been quite some time, Father."

Cold and distant for as long as Athrun could remember, his father didn't so much as nod. But then, he had a lot on his mind. Patrick Zala was the National Defense Committee Chairman of the Supreme Council for ZAFT. While growing up, Athrun had barely seen him.

As the shuttle drove off, Zala looked at Creuset and said, "I agree with the opinions in your report." He tapped a set of papers against his lap. "The problem is, the mobile suits have been developed with such efficiency that *anybody* can pilot them. I've deleted mention of that."

Athrun looked up in surprise.

His father returned his gaze. "But then there's the fact that the pilot of the enemy machine *isn't* just anybody—he's a Coordinator. That sort of information will just cause the moderates to argue endlessly." He addressed Athrun, "I suppose you were reluctant to report that your friend had jumped the fence, eh?"

Athrun's heart panged as his father continued.

"So. They've developed a mobile suit versatile enough that even a Natural can operate it now. I'll put that back in and we'll leave it at that. Do you understand, Athrun?"

"Y-yes," he replied. He understood his father's tenuous position, but such political scheming just felt undeniably dirty, and didn't help Athrun feel any better about joining ZAFT. He had always spoken out against war. Now he was the one wielding a gun. Kira wasn't wrong to be furious with him; he'd said he was fighting to protect his Natural friends, but whom was Athrun protecting? Whom could Athrun call a friend?

The shuttle slowly approached Aprilius One, the city that housed the Supreme Council. Athrun had never felt so alone.

> > > > >

Far away, the Archangel shot through space. "It's confirmed," Tonomura said. "No sign of the enemy within a three thousand mile radius. We've lost 'em."

Everyone breathed a sigh of relief – except Murrue. Their problems were far from over and she knew it. They had no supplies. It was a long journey to the moon base. They were going to run out of water way before then. Still, she masked her concerns and played the role of confident leader.

La Flaga went to Murrue's side and quietly asked, "How bad is it?"

She should have known he could see right through her. "We have emergency rations, but the real problem is ammo and water. If the refugees cooperate and we ration, we'll be fine."

He nodded, but they both knew better. They had to reach that moon, fast.

She called up the navigation course on the monitor, disappointed with what she saw. "This is our path at full speed? Can't we take a more direct route?"

Natarle shook her head. "No use. If we orbit any closer to Earth, we'll enter the debris belt."

Murrue mused, "Seems like we could save time if we just plowed right through the belt, then."

"At this speed," Neumann said wryly, "if we went in, this ship would become just another hunk of junk."

The debris belt was a zone where Earth dumped its garbage. Since humans began interstellar travel and abandoned their satellite stations, shuttlecraft and all manner of refuse had been discarded in space. The trashy graveyard that floated around Earth's orbit was a lethal obstacle course.

The Hawk of Endymion glanced at Murrue suddenly and beamed. "Just a second," he said. "Debris . . ." His smile widened. "Am I the man who can make the impossible *possible*, or what?" He winked.

> > > > >

Bathed in sunlight, Athrun and Creuset rode a glass elevator from the docking bay down to the New Century colony. It was a thirty-seven mile drop. The commander read his computer's data while Athrun gazed out at the scenery. They cleared the clouds and the city of Aprilius One suddenly came into view. A blue sea sparkled. Green islands peaked in the distance. After weeks spent cooped up in a battleship, the view was a sight for sore eyes. It was . . . home.

The elevator monitor switched from a music video to a news program. "Supreme Council Chairman Clyne issued a proclamation last night that mourning ceremonies for Junius Seven will be held in one week."

Athrun and Creuset both stared at the screen. The footage showed the chairman, a man in his late forties, with a long jaw and gentle features. Beside him stood a pretty girl, her long wavy hair dyed a soft pink, providing a nice contrast to her lily-white skin. Athrun's eyes were drawn to her—Lacus Clyne—the chairman's daughter, famous pop idol of the PLANT colonies.

Creuset examined him with interest. "Isn't that your fiancée?" he asked.

Athrun's eyes flicked down. Their engagement was well publicized; still, it felt odd to talk about it with the commander. Everyone around him just assumed he and Lacus would marry soon. He didn't dislike her, of course;

she was a wonderful girl. She looked so delicate that Athrun wanted to protect her. But marriage . . . ? He just didn't see it happening.

"Isn't the young lady going to be a representative at the next memorial service?" Creuset asked with odd cheer. "How wonderful."

Did the commander not notice Athrun's discomfort? Or did he simply fail to care? It couldn't be that Creuset was teasing him, could it?

Creuset looked at Athrun from the corner of his eye. "Your marriage will unite the families of Secretary Zala and Chairman Clyne. The next generation of Coordinators will have a brilliant future. I'm looking forward to it."

"Thank you." Athrun bowed his head awkwardly. The compliment felt hollow—just as he did.

> > > > >

Inside the Archangel's hangar, Kira made the final adjustments to the Strike. La Flaga had given him specific advice: a mobile suit pilot should never entrust his machine to anyone else. Kira finished his work and sighed.

"I'm so tired . . ." He went to the mess hall to grab a bite to eat before taking a nap. Rationing made for bland menus and small portions, but at least everyone had enough to go around. Tolle and Miriallia sat at a table, laughing. Next to them, Sai and Flay ate quietly. Kira approached them slowly, noticing that Sai gave Flay a little nudge.

She got up and looked right into Kira's eyes. "Uh . . . um, Kira?" She bowed. "Sorry about before."

Embarrassed, he said, "Huh? Wh-what?"

Tolle added, "You know. When she ratted you out on Artemis?"

The memory returned, sharp and harsh. *And he's a Coordinator.* Kira's face hardened for a moment, but he forced himself to smile.

"It's all right. I'm not angry. It's the truth anyway."

Flay looked instantly relieved. "Thanks." She smiled at Sai. Those two certainly were intimate lately.

"So, here you are!" Maintenance Officer Murdoch said, walking into the room, his boots clomping on the tiled floor. "The captain wants to see y'all."

> > > > >

This wasn't going well, La Flaga thought. He felt sorry for Murrue, he really did. These kids weren't exactly thrilled about having to go get their own supplies . . .

"Where are we gonna get them?" they asked.

He shifted his weight. "Yeah. When we say 'get' we mean . . . find."

Murrue sighed. "We're approaching the debris belt."

"The debris belt?" Kira asked. The students looked at one another.

Sai did a double-take. "Now wait just a minute! You can't mean—"

"You're quick, four-eyes," La Flaga said, patting Sai's shoulder. "Time to take out the trash."

Murrue frowned at him. She looked cute when annoyed. "It's not just trash. There are all kinds of things in the belt that could be useful. For instance, there are fully stocked ships out there that went down in battle. But their parts still work."

Kira looked a little creeped out. "You want us to go on those ghost ships?"

"What else can we do?" La Flaga said seriously. "Unless you've got a better idea, we're not gonna last much longer."

The students' expressions turned sour.

"I'm going to need your help with piloting the pods," Murrue said to them. La Flaga could tell that she had strong reservations with his plan, but it was the only plan they had. "We don't intend to disturb the dead," she continued. "We'll only take what we need to go on living." She spoke firmly, but under that veil of authority, La Flaga saw her self-doubt. And as for this latest little scheme, she clearly didn't like the idea of grave robbing any more than the kids did.

La Flaga, for his part, had no qualms playing trash collector if it meant this ship would survive.

> > > > >

The PLANT colonies were comprised of twelve capitol cities that specialized in their own field of research. These capitols each elected a member to the Supreme Council; twelve officials decided the fate of the PLANTs and their inhabitants. Athrun and Creuset now stood before the council's table. Seated at the center of the semi-circle was Chairman Siegel Clyne.

Just as Athrun's father was a member of the council, so too were Yzak's, Nicol's and Dearka's fathers. (The young soldiers excelled on their own merits, of course, but Athrun was always aware of the influence the pilots' families had on ZAFT.)

The council sat and listened intensely as Commander Creuset gave his report. "I think you understand," the blond man said respectfully, "after hearing about the course of events, that our mission never once constituted an attack on Heliopolis. We never had any such intention. Rather, the destruction of the colony rests squarely on the Earth Force's shoulders; the Central Shaft was crippled by their own fire power."

Athrun doubted the commander believed what he was saying. After all, the man had ordered the use of Equipment D—how could he not have foreseen Heliopolis' demise? It didn't add up and yet the council jumped on the bandwagon.

"After all, Orb sided with the Earth Force in secret!" one councilor said. "They ignored the treaty first."

"But, Councilor Athha, is this the image we Coordinators want to project?"

"Look, are you really going to take the word of someone who lives on Earth against one of our own commanders?"

The debate spilled out of the room and echoed into the hall. Suddenly, Patrick Zala's voice rang out, "Commander Creuset. Were the Earth Force mobile suits really worth all the lives it cost to get them?"

Clearly, Creuset had been waiting for that question. He smiled. "Regarding the mobile suits' capabilities, I would like to call on Athrun Zala to report. He had actual combat experience in one of the X Numbers, fighting against the only suit we could not capture."

Athrun felt like an actor at an audition. He stood up straight as an image of his mobile suit appeared on the screen behind him. "This is the Aegis, retrieved from Heliopolis." He switched to an image of the Aegis in battle—murmurs of interest bounced around the room.

He continued his report, stiffly, like an amateur actor. After all, that's what he was. More than once, Chairman Clyne glanced at Secretary Zala with an incredulous expression. It made Athrun nervous. He discussed the Earth's Gundams. "As our data suggests, its abilities exceed those of our next generation fleet, the CGUE, which are almost ready for deployment. In conclusion," he took a deep breath, "I believe Commander Creuset's assessment of the situation is correct."

The minute he was finished, Athrun took his seat. The councilors looked worried.

"To build such a thing—and Naturals, at that."

"But aren't they still just in the experimental stage? They've only made five, right?"

"If they've gone this far, they must be ready for mass production. Should we wait until then before we do something?"

So, Athrun thought, this is what fans the flames of war: fear. Maybe it was because they had been persecuted for so many years. Maybe it was because a Coordinator's mind couldn't fathom a Natural's illogical, unpredictable behavior. Maybe, deep down, their superior race always felt inferior to their creators. Whatever the reason, Athrun realized this war would not be over any time soon.

"Clearly they intend to attack the PLANTs!"

"But does it mean we must keep fighting? Our numbers are already dwindling."

"Now is not the appropriate time to discuss such things. We must act!"

Athrun watched as his father and Commander Creuset shared a look. The two of them had managed to set the council's anxiety and resentment ablaze.

"Silence! Silence!" Patrick Zala boomed. The hall quieted. "Nobody wants to fight. Peace is our deepest wish." Everyone nodded in agreement as his father continued, "But who smashed that dream? Who, greedy for power, bound us to lives of misery? Slavery? Who *slaughtered* us?" Secretary Zala's stare burned right through Athrun. "Remember Junius Seven! Remember the Bloody Valentine!"

> > > > >

"That's a destroyer," Sai said, pointing to the screen of his pod. "Its engine is toast." He nudged Officer Pal toward the shuttle's monitor. Scraps of ships floated all around them.

"It's not too bad," Officer Pal murmured. "We can probably salvage some ammunition."

The students' psychological resistance to grave robbing faded fast under the thrill of the hunt. The officers, however, sobered. "I hope the people on board escaped all right," Officer Pal said under his breath.

Nearby, Tolle and Miriallia advanced their pod through the ocean of debris, ascending over a large spaceship. Beyond it laid an interstellar junkyard. They gasped.

Acres of frozen ground stretched before their eyes— fields of farmland from a former PLANT colony that had hardened into shards of ice in the cold of space.

Underneath the stiff sheets of water, plantation houses and buildings stood intact. High above those, the colony's Central Shaft had snapped in two pieces; self-repairing glass, high-tension wires, and chunks of the outer wall floated in clusters over it, looking like the broken bones of a mangled skeleton.

The students approached the ground carefully, making their way to a large building that looked like a shelter. Miriallia opened the door . . . and screamed. Tolle stood beside her, paralyzed with awe—the rotting corpse of a woman, shielding her infant in her arms, floated past them. A cloth teddy bear was suspended in the zero gravity, torn, missing an eye. It was horrific.

The students didn't understand that they'd stumbled upon the massacre of Junius Seven.

> > > > >

La Flaga watched the kid on the bridge of the Archangel as Kira looked at Natarle like she'd lost her mind. "That water? Out there? Are you crazy?" he said.

"There's close to a hundred million tons of frozen water," she replied coldly. "And we haven't found any other sources of H2O yet." They'd already decided to transport the frozen water from the remains of Junius Seven. Now, the task of convincing Kira to help out fell to La Flaga.

"Kira—" he started.

"You saw them, didn't you?" the boy pressed. "You *saw* them. Hundreds of thousands of people died in that PLANT!"

He watched Kira's face—it must have been an especially hard thing for the kid, what with being a Coordinator and all. But La Flaga wasn't going to let the crew die of thirst while there was a viable source of water nearby.

"No one wants to intrude on their memories, Kira," he said. "If there was any other way . . . It can't be helped. *We're* alive. We have to keep on going. And to do that, we need your help." Once again, appealing to the boy's protective nature did the trick.

Resigned, Kira nodded.

> > > > >

"Two hundred, forty-three thousand, seven hundred and twenty-one people died on that awful day," Patrick Zala reminded the council. "Among them was Lenore Zala, my wife."

The council members nodded. PLANT colonies had acted as the Earth's harvest stations for raw interstellar materials. Their inhabitants, the exiled Coordinators, had been forced to produce the Earth's energy and industrial goods without ever getting to share in the profits. They were essentially treated like slaves.

But the Coordinators were so intelligent, agile, and intuitive—their spirit could not accept such disdainful treatment for long. As the relationship between the PLANTs and the Earth worsened, Coordinators cut off the flow of goods to Earth. In return, Earth shut off their food supply—by firing a nuclear missile at the sole food-producing colony: Junius Seven. In a single instant, the entire city was destroyed. Since then, the Coordinators developed neutron jammers to hinder further nuclear attacks. But the fear of another massacre always weighed heavily on their minds.

"Instead of providing the bare minimum for our survival," Zala continued, "which would have ended hostilities, they sent us total annihilation. *Genocide*. Well . . . the Naturals have acted in vain. They can break our hearts, my friends, but they can never take our will to be free!"

The debate ended with a cacophony of applause.

Athrun walked down a corridor adjacent to the council chamber, stopping for a moment to look at the Evidence 1 monument. Nicknamed the Whale Rock, the huge fossil hung like a piece of artwork on the wall. It displayed the skeletal remains of an aquatic creature with wings extending out of its back. Found in CE 18 on a meteor that had crashed into Jupiter, Evidence 1 had been regarded as the first tangible proof of extraterrestrial life. It was a source of great controversy back on Earth.

"Athrun," a kind voice called.

Seeing it was Chairman Clyne, Athrun stood at attention out of reflex. "Your Excellency, Chairman Clyne." He saluted.

"Don't greet me like a stranger, son," said the chairman.

"Well, uh . . ." Athrun lowered his head. They shared a smile.

Clyne looked at the Whale Rock for a moment, deep in thought. "You've finally come back, but Lacus is away on business. Good grief. When are the two of you ever going to find the time to get together?"

"Yes, I know. I'm very sorry." Athrun bowed.

Clyne laughed again. "No, it's not necessary to apologize to me. You are just doing your duty." He glanced back at the council hall for a moment. "It's likely to get worse before it gets better. I understand the points your father made, but . . ." Tired wrinkles on the man's face seemed to sag with sadness. Siegel Clyne was a moderate; he was gentle and patient and the exact opposite of Patrick Zala. It was almost like comparing a dove to a hawk. For the past year, Clyne had opposed Patrick Zala and the other radicals, working hard to negotiate with Earth. It was a heavy burden.

Commander Creuset came out of the chamber with the elder Zala. He approached and rattled off a salute to the Chairman.

Patrick Zala dismissed at the commander sternly. "Follow the Earth Force's new battleship and its mobile suit," he ordered. "The Lacony and Porto teams will be under my command. You'll leave port in seventy-two hours."

"Yes, sir," Creuset said. "With your permission, Excellency." He bowed—shooting a look to Athrun—and then turned to go. Athrun saluted and followed the commander out of the hall.

> > > > >

An alarm blared in the Strike's cockpit. Kira looked up at his monitor, startled. Beyond the debris, a large heat-source was closing in. He checked his readings—it was a reconnaissance GINN mobile suit.

"What are they doing in a place like this?" he wondered. The Archangel hadn't finished loading supplies. If the GINN spotted them now and called for backup, they were done for.

Kira pulled the beam rifle's target scope down. He honed in on the GINN, watching as it appeared to search for something. Kira locked on target and held his breath. "Leave," he whispered. "Please just go." His finger squeezed the trigger.

As if it had heard Kira, the GINN lit its vernier thrusters and pulled out. It stopped again—turned—and spotted one of the students' collector pods.

"Idiot!" he shouted. "Why couldn't you just go?!"

The GINN hefted its rifle and fired a shot, grazing the pod. Kira pulled the trigger. A single beam pierced through the GINN's fuselage, exploding it.

Kuzzey's voice came over the intercom, "Whoa. Thanks, Kira! I thought I was gonna bite the dust for a—"

"Strike, what happened?" the Archangel's call overlapped Kuzzey.

Without answering, Kira flipped the communications switch off. He had just killed one of his fellow Coordinators. He *was* a traitor.

No one here wants to fight. We do what we have to, to protect the ones we love.

The alarm sounded again. Except this time, it was neither a mobile suit nor a battleship. Checking his data, he saw that it was an escape pod, floating haphazardly near the Strike. But what was an escape pod doing all the way out here? Cocking his head to the side, Kira moved the mobile suit's hands, picking up the vessel as if it were a toy.

> > > > >

Natarle glared at Kira as he got out of the cockpit and jumped onto the hangar floor. "You seem to have a nasty habit of picking up strays," she admonished.

Kira didn't respond.

The rescue pod rocked on its side next to the Strike. Captain Murrue and La Flaga exchanged looks and sighed. Officer Murdoch went over to it. "I'll crack 'er open," he said, starting in on the locks.

Whoosh!

The hatch opened almost immediately. Soldiers lifted their guns and took aim at . . . a tiny pink robo-pet with long ears and two large, round eyes. "Haro! Haro!" it chirped. Everyone stared.

Then, a soft voice drifted out to them. "Thank you. Thank you so much for helping me."

Kira's eyes riveted to the young girl coming out of the escape pod. She had long pink hair and wore a fetching white dress with lavender trim. She looked about the same age as Kira. Her skin was smooth and white as ivory; her smile was gentle and kind. She floated out of the pod and hovered at zero gravity, lovely and ethereal. Kira was mesmerized.

She kept on floating above their heads. Kira snapped to and jumped up, grabbing the girl's slight wrist and bringing her safely to the floor. "Thank you," she said, smiling up at him with ice-blue eyes. Kira blushed hotly.

The girl's pretty face suddenly looked puzzled. She glanced around, her eyes resting on Kira's uniform with the Earth Alliance Force insignia. She swallowed. "So, this isn't a ZAFT ship, I take it?"

Natarle bit her lip and let out a long sigh.

Athrun knelt quietly at his mother's grave. He watched as loose petals from the bouquet he'd brought blew away in the breeze. He stared at the headstone: Lenore Zala, CE 33–70. As with all the other victims of the Bloody Valentine, the headstone was merely a symbolic marker with no body buried beneath.

Lenore Zala was an agricultural researcher working on the colony at the time of the attack. Athrun had not spent much time with his mother, but she'd always showered him with love and affection when he did get to see her. He missed her during those research trips. His father was never around, either, but he understood their work was important.

Then, in one instant, she'd been irrevocably torn away from him.

We fight to protect ourselves; we fight for freedom—his father had said that. If they waited for it, peace would never come. The Naturals certainly wouldn't hand it to them. If he were to shout to the heavens that he abhorred war, would that make the conflict disappear? No.

No, he had to fight. He had to *win*.

> > > > >

A crowd formed at the door of the interrogation room. Kira wrestled with Tolle, trying to press his ear to the door and listen in on the conversation in the next room. Sai and Kuzzey pushed in from behind, squeezing between Officers Tonomura and Pal, who tried to look nonchalant as they hovered around the door's edge.

"Hey, don't push."

"Can you hear anything?"

"What're they saying?"

The door swung open and they fell like a stack of dominos. Natarle stared coldly at the boys on the floor. "You have supplies to restock! Get back to your posts!"

The boys ran off. Kira lingered for a moment, catching a glimpse of the pink-haired girl. She saw him and waved. He blushed and high-tailed it out of there.

> > > > >

Grinning at Kira, La Flaga closed the door. Murrue cleared her throat. "Excuse my crew, they're new. Now then, where were we?"

The girl nodded. "I'm Lacus Clyne. And this is my friend, Haro." She held up the pink robo-pet. "Haro!" it insisted.

La Flaga palmed his face while Murrue and Natarle could only sigh. Suddenly La Flaga looked sharply at the girl. "Clyne? As in, *Supreme Council Chairman*, Clyne?"

Lacus clasped her hands together and nodded enthusiastically. "Yes! He's my father! Do you know him?"

All three Earth Force officers' shoulders slumped. Was she teasing them? Or did she just not have a clue? "Ah, never mind," La Flaga said, smoothing over his surprise. He stood up straight and crossed his arms. It was *her* interrogation, not his. "What happened out there? Why are you in an escape pod?"

Lacus looked sad. "I came with a small crew to take a survey for the Junius Seven memorial ceremony." Murrue leaned forward intently and encouraged her to continue. "We encountered an Earth Force ship. They said they had to make an official inspection, so I allowed them to board. For some reason, they took great offense at our mission. Harsh words were said and there was a struggle; a fight broke out." She shuddered. "It was terrible."

La Flaga exchanged looks with Murrue.

The girl frowned. "No one had done anything, you understand. The Earth Force people should have kept calm, but they wouldn't. I ordered those around me to get into escape pods. I hope they made it okay."

La Flaga bit his tongue. He knew that a civilian ship had recently been shot down in the area, but he wasn't going to upset this young lady with that news. Their immediate questions answered, the officers got up to give Lacus some privacy.

The Hawk of Endymion watched as the girl approached the chamber window and took in the sight of Junius Seven's wreckage. She hugged her robo-pet close and whispered, "Let's pray, Haro, that they may rest in peace." Ashamed, La Flaga quietly closed the door.

A few hours later, the Archangel finished storing supplies and was ready to launch. La Flaga insisted on a brief moment of silence for the victims of the Bloody Valentine. Miriallia had thousands of little paper flowers that the students had made released over the debris.

The crew bowed their heads out of respect, and then on Murrue's order, the Archangel sped toward the moon.

> > > > >

As Athrun made his way to the Vesalius, he was surprised to see his father standing so close to Commander Creuset. They were talking. Could this be the first time Patrick Zala had ever come to see his son off? Or were they simply discussing last minute battle plans?

"Athrun," his father said. "Have you heard about Miss Lacus?"

Athrun cocked his head. Was this something to do with the ceremony, or perhaps Lacus' new hit album? "No. Why?"

His father said nothing, so Commander Creuset spoke up, "The survey ship that went to Junius Seven to prepare for the memorial service . . . it's been destroyed."

Athrun's eyes widened. Lacus had been aboard that ship. Would his father now change their mission? "Commander," he said steadily, "do you intend to involve the Vesalius?"

"Ho," Creuset chuckled. "You're a cold fish, aren't you, dear boy?" The blond straightened. "Of course we're going to look for her."

Athrun frowned. "But it's a small civilian ship and we don't even know if there are any survivors. Isn't it a bit unusual to deploy a Nazca-class—"

Commander Creuset interrupted, "Athrun. The Yun Lo team sent a GINN to look for the escape pod. It hasn't returned. We fear the worst." Athrun listened grimly as the blond man continued. "Junius Seven has been pulled into the debris belt by strong G-forces. It's a dangerous location—anything could be out there."

Junius Seven was close to Earth. It didn't mean, however, that the Earth Force was crawling around out there, looking to target civilian ships. It just didn't make sense.

Patrick Zala spoke firmly, "It's well known throughout the PLANTs that Miss Lacus is your fiancée. There's no reason for your team to delay, Athrun." He put an awkward hand on Athrun's shoulder. "She's one of a kind. Go take care of her."

Athrun frowned as his father turned and walked away. He peered up at Creuset and mumbled bitterly, "So now I'm supposed to rescue her and return the conquering hero, huh?"

The commander let out a silky laugh and squeezed his shoulder. "Or else come back wailing your head off, clutching her corpse." Creuset sported a thin smile. "Either makes a better story for Chairman Clyne than if you did nothing. If you don't want to go for Lacus' sake, go for his." He extended his hand for Athrun to board the ship first.

> > > > >

Kira approached the commissary, startled to hear Flay's high-pitched voice shout, "I hate her! I hate her!"

"Flay, what's wrong with you?" Miriallia asked.

Kira walked in, nodding to Kuzzey. "What's up?"

"Miriallia asked Flay to take a meal to that girl you picked up. It set her off."

Flay stomped her foot. "I hate her! I'm afraid to go into that Coordinator's room!"

"Flay!" Miriallia rebuked sharply.

The redheaded girl looked up at Kira and stuttered, "O-of course, Kira is different. But that girl's from ZAFT! She has Coordinator reflexes! She could kill us all!"

Oddly enough, Kira agreed with her. That girl could snap Flay's neck if she wanted to and he knew it. But he held his tongue as Kuzzey responded, "I don't think she's going to come flying at you from across the room or anything, Flay."

"How do you know?" Flay demanded.

A soft voice drifted into the mess hall, "Who's going to fly at whom?"

Kira spun around—there stood Lacus herself, smiling. Everybody froze.

"Oh, did I startle you? Sorry." She bowed. "I'm so thirsty. And to be honest, though I know it's unladylike, I have to admit I'm starving. Is this the commissary? I'd love to get a little something, if that's okay . . ."

"Hang on," Kuzzey said, "Wasn't your door locked?"

Flay chimed in, "How does a ZAFT girl get to just walk around here wherever she wants?"

Lacus retained her gracious expression. "I asked properly if it was all right to go out."

Kira frowned. "And they said it was okay?"

"Well, no one answered me," she replied. "I asked three times, and then finally I figured no one would mind."

Kuzzey smacked his forehead.

Lacus stepped up to Flay and extended her hand. "Anyway, I'm not in ZAFT. ZAFT is the name of the army. I'm just a civilian."

"B-but it's the same thing!" Flay insisted, stepping back. "You're a Coordinator!"

"Yes, I am a Coordinator," Lacus said slowly, as if speaking to a child. "But that doesn't mean I'm in the army. You're a Natural, but you're not in the army, are you? It's the same with me. We're not so different." She offered her hand again, giving Flay a soft smile.

Flay smacked Lacus' arm down. "No! Why should I?" Hatred poured out of her voice. "Don't try to be friends with me—Coordinator!"

Kira sucked in a breath. Flay's anger and uncouth behavior toward an innocent girl, simply because she was a Coodinator, cut him to the quick. They couldn't change who they were. And no amount of kindness on their part would convince Flay otherwise.

Kira felt a cold kind of despair sink into his chest.

> > > > >

Murrue watched as La Flaga sauntered up to her on the bridge. "Well, just when we think the coast is clear, we get a pink princess." He rubbed his temples. "I don't remember you asking for one of those."

She bit her lip. He always talked to her as if *she* were the subordinate officer. It took her a while to get used to his casual personality. He seemed like an irresponsible slacker, but in truth, he was the most dependable man she'd ever met. She'd already lost count of how many times he'd saved their lives. Murrue wondered if he was just putting up a front in order to keep her and the crew calm. If so, she appreciated the effort. He must be exhausted.

She shrugged. "I guess all we can do is take her with us to the moon base."

"Isn't there another port along the way?" he pressed.

"Yes, but at the moon base, we'll—"

"Murrue," he cut her off. She blinked. "You think they're gonna give her a warm welcome?" He raised an eyebrow at her, his point sinking in. The daughter of the PLANTs' ruler would be treated as a bargaining chip and nothing more.

"I don't want anything to happen to her, of course," Murrue clarified. It was important that La Flaga not get the wrong idea about her. "She's a civilian and a child to boot."

Behind them, Natarle scoffed. "What about them?" She indicated Tolle in the co-pilot's seat. "They're children and civilians, too, but you've got them piloting a battleship and fighting in the field."

Murrue felt suddenly tired. "Ensign Badgiruel, that's enough," she growled, pinching the bridge of her nose.

"We pulled the Heliopolis kids into the war, but now you're saying we should exclude that girl?" Natarle said, raising her voice. "She's Chairman Clyne's daughter—she's no ordinary Coordinator!"

Murrue knew it well. Such a hostage might even prove useful in stopping the war altogether. Her instincts told her that to even think that way was wrong; but Natarle was a seasoned officer and seemed quite insistent. Maybe Natarle knew better.

> > > > >

Lacus sat in the interrogation room where she had been originally confined. She sighed, looking at the handsome young man that stood beside the door. "I really have to stay in here again?"

"Yes," he said, giving her a forced smile as he handed her a tray of food.

She pouted. "I wish I could eat out there and get to know everybody."

The boy averted his eyes. "This is an Earth Alliance Force ship, you know . . . Well, there are a lot of people here who don't like Coordinators very much." He shivered a little. "What I mean is, technically, we're enemies. It can't be helped."

"That's a shame," she said, matching his sad expression. She gave him her best smile and touched the sleeve of his shirt. "But you have been very kind to me. Thank you."

"I—" He startled, surprised. "It's because . . . I'm a Coordinator, too."

Lacus nodded. Of course he was; she could sense it. "You are kind because you are *you.*" Finally, the boy smiled. "What's your name?"

"Ah, Kira. Kira Yamato."

"I see. Thank you, Mister Kira."

"N-no. Kira's just fine."

"Thank you, Kira."

The boy blushed.

> > > > >

Back in the mess hall, Kuzzey sat at the table across from Flay and Miriallia. "Are you in Blue Cosmos?" he asked the redhead.

Blue Cosmos was a religious sect militantly persecuting Coordinators by advocating strict Naturalism. During the boom of genetic engineering, Blue Cosmos turned to terrorism and piracy.

"No," Flay retorted. She paused and swallowed. "But their cause isn't so wrong. There're people out there with tampered genes. They go against the laws of nature. They're a mistake!" She peered at Miriallia and Kuzzey. "I mean, don't you agree?"

Kuzzey pushed his food around his plate. Part of him agreed with her. "But you're forgetting something," he said quietly. "Kira's a Coordinator, too. And if he hadn't piloted that Gundam, we'd be dead."

Kira had saved his life just hours before, striking down a Coordinator GINN in order to protect his collector pod. Even so, when he thought about Kira always getting special treatment, operating the super cool X Number—he couldn't help but feel a little jealous. After all, every time Kira did something amazing, it only reminded him of his own limitations.

Kira closed Lacus' door and headed down the hall. Along the way, he met up with Sai.

"I heard about what happened from Miriallia," the older boy said. "Don't mind Flay. You know, it's just with everything . . . I'll talk to her when she cools off."

With Sai always having to defend Flay, he was acting more and more like a lawyer and less and less like a boyfriend. Until Kira had heard about the love letter, he'd never imagined the two of them together. It was an odd pairing to begin with.

They rounded the corner; a clear, gorgeous sound drifted down the hallway and wriggled up Kira's spine. He cocked his head to listen—it was Lacus. Lacus was singing. She was a pop star, after all. Now he could understand why she was so famous.

"That's really pretty," he murmured.

Sai nodded. They listened at the door, entranced. "I guess she got that talent from her altered genes, too, huh?"

Kira blinked—the magic of the moment had been broken.

> > > > >

Officer Pal sat at his communications station on the bridge, sipping hot tea, when an urgent message came through. He spit out his drink and then had to fumble with cleaning the gauges and monitor. "C-Captain!" he called out.

Murrue and Natarle turned. "What is it?" Murrue asked.

"An encoded message! From the Eighth Fleet!"

"Can you trace it?"

"Already there," he responded. The two women stood beside him, peering at his monitor. A unique wave signature gyrated on screen. "Almost got it," he said, fingers pounding over the keyboard. Before long, a voice cracked through the speakers.

"This . . . Eighth Fleet vanguard . . . Montgomery. Archangel . . . in!"

Excitement rippled through the bridge. "It's Commodore Halberton's force." Pal said.

"What's their position?" Murrue asked.

"Hold on," Pal responded. "It's still very distant."

"We can join them," Murrue continued.

Tonomura and Neumann gave each other high-fives. So far they had been on their own, desperate to make it home in one piece. Now there was some hope. The crew smiled—just a little more patience and they'd be able to make it to the moon base and catch up with their families.

As news broke out on the ship, the refugees gave a happy cheer. Flay hugged Sai close, brightening. "Papa!"

"He'll be with the fleet," Sai told her. "We sent over the ship's roster, so he knows you're on board." He smiled. She looked so happy.

Only one person did not rejoice: Lacus. She sat in her room, holding Haro close, silently wondering what would happen to her now.

On the bridge, the signal from the Montgomery finally came in loud and clear. Captain Copeman said, "Our ships will wait here to rendezvous with you at which time the Archangel will fall under our command. We will join the rest of the fleet and escort you to the moon base. Everyone here prays for your safe arrival."

Murrue sagged with relief. It was good to be back in the fold.

Another man came on screen; he was middle-aged, wore an expensive suit, and carried himself with an air of authority. "Atlantic Federation Undersecretary, George Allster," he introduced himself. "First and foremost, may I thank you for all your efforts in rescuing the civilians of Heliopolis."

She recognized the name—Allster—Flay's father. Now that she thought about it, rescuing the beloved daughter of one of the highest-ranking government officials might not have been such a bad call after all. She owed Kira one.

Allster got right up in the camera lens. "My daughter was on your crew roster. I'd like to see her if I could, please."

Captain Copeman interrupted, "Mister Undersecretary, we'll certainly arrange that right after we rendezvous. Don't worry, it won't be long now."

Sai smiled from his operation's seat. "Undersecretary or not, he's still a father."

> > > > >

Meanwhile, the Vesalius, charged with finding Lacus Clyne and bringing her safely home, caught sight of the Eighth Fleet on their radar screens.

Captain Ades mused, "What is the Earth Force doing all the way out here?"

Looking at the radar panel, Creuset stroked his chin. "What will the Paw do if it does reach the moon?" The Paw was the name that ZAFT had given to the Archangel, due to the way its gunwales looked like the clawed foot of a massive beast.

Ades speculated, "Re-supply? Or join their fleet?"

"The Lacony and Port are moving in more slowly than I expected," Creuset said. "If the Naturals mean to re-supply, we can't simply let them go."

"We can't?" Ades asked, perplexed.

They had one ship up against an entire fleet; it was no joking matter. Creuset wore his trademark expression—a thin, condescending smile—so Ades couldn't begin to fathom what the man was thinking.

"We're soldiers," Creuset said. "Though our mission is to look for Miss Lacus, we cannot overlook this opportunity to cripple the enemy merely for the sake of one young girl. I won't go down in history as a laughingstock."

> > > > >

The Earth Force's Montgomery finally appeared on the Archangel's radar. Happy murmurs filled the bridge. Officer Pal, however, did not join in the merriment. Bending over his radar screen, he frowned. He adjusted his gauges, but the electronic noises only got worse. "This is just like ..."

Murrue glanced over at him, worried. "What's wrong?"

"It's jammers! The whole area is being hit with interference!" They'd been spotted by the enemy.

> > > > >

The Eighth Fleet's Montgomery had also detected the ZAFT ship. An officer at the control station shouted, "Heat sources approaching! Four mobile suits, three GINNs." He checked his instruments. "The last one . . . it's the Aegis. The X303 Aegis!"

Captain Copeman held his breath for a moment, then bellowed orders. "Send a message to the Archangel, tell them to retreat! Launch our mobile armors! Move!"

Undersecretary Allster protested, "Why bother going into the fray, if we can't even rendezvous with the Archangel?"

The captain shot him a glare. "If we don't go in, the Archangel will be sunk."

> > > > >

Murrue could not believe what she was hearing. "The Aegis?" She closed her eyes and clenched her fists. "From that Nazca-class *again?*"

"Affirmative," Pal answered. "Captain, there's a message from the Montgomery: Rendezvous cancelled. Archangel—retreat."

Sai lurched forward. "But we need that fleet. And what about Flay's father?"

She looked down, her judgment clouded. Murrue happily anticipated joining the fleet and going back to *taking* orders, instead of *giving* them. But right now, she didn't have a choice—the crew depended on her. "If we reverse course now, there's no guarantee we'll escape. Go to battle stations! Archangel, continue advancing toward the fleet!"

> > > > >

Klaxons blared. Kira flew out of his guest quarters and ran for the locker room. Along the way, he passed in front of Lacus' room—the door was open again. She peeked out and whispered to Kira, "What's going on?"

"Battle prep. Please get back inside," he said urgently.

"Battle prep? There's going to be a fight?"

"It's already started," he said, gently grabbing her arms and pushing her back in the room.

"Are you going to fight too, Kira?"

Looking into those ice-blue eyes, he struggled to find the right words. "Please, just don't go anywhere. It's important you stay here. Okay?" Kira firmly nudged her back and locked her door.

He turned to run when someone caught him by the arm and spun him around forcefully. "Kira!" Flay called anxiously. "What's this about a battle? What about Papa's ship?"

Papa's . . . ship? He couldn't think straight with the object of his affections clinging to him so desperately. Tears formed at the corners of her eyes. It pained him.

"Please just tell me everything will be all right?" She sniffed. "Papa's ship won't be destroyed, right?"

He didn't have time. He had to get out there. But he took a deep breath and said, "Yeah, Flay. Everything's gonna be okay. Don't worry. I'll be out there." He smiled reassuringly and squeezed her hand before removing it from his arm.

Then he ran down the hall, ripping his clothes off as he made his way to the locker room. He changed into his pilot suit and dashed into the hangar bay. La Flaga's Zero was already launching without him.

"You're late, boy!" Murdoch bellowed at him.

"Sorry!" Kira yelled over his shoulder as he climbed into the cockpit.

He brought up the systems as Miriallia briefed him on the situation. "It's that Nazca-class ship and three GINNs . . . and the Aegis. Watch yourself out there, Kira."

Kira's hands paused over the controls. The Aegis?

Sai's worried voice came over the intercom. "Hey, Kira? Flay's father is in the vanguard ship, the Montgomery. Please, watch over them."

Ah. So that was what Flay was babbling about. Great. No pressure or anything. He advanced the Strike to the launch pad with a sense of foreboding.

> > > > >

Athrun flew his mobile suit between the battleships. He wanted to confirm whether Lacus was alive or dead and have done with it. The last thing he needed was to fight Kira . . .

"Athrun!" a comrade from a GINN hailed him. "Show us what your fancy toy can do!"

Three mobile armors launched from the Earth Force's vanguard ship and immediately shot missiles at him. The Aegis swiftly dodged and cut the rockets down. He hefted his beam rifle and fired a single shot—the laser ripped through all three Moebiuses simultaneously. Athrun was an excellent marksman and the Aegis' power was staggering.

He pressed on and as soon as he was in range, he fired at the first ship in his sights. Engines down, the enemy dropped out of battle.

> > > > >

Aboard the Montgomery, an officer called out, "Escort ship Barnard is silent! X303 is now approaching the Rowe!"

Undersecretary Allster's jaw hung open. "The Barnard, defeated? By our own machine? Impossible!" He watched in disbelief as a GINN closed the distance. A Moebius tried to block the enemy's approach, but it was shot down. On its descent, the Moebius managed to shoot the GINN's side out —it exploded in a ball of fire.

Through the burst, the Archangel emerged. Allster said joyfully, "They've come!"

Captain Copeman balled his hands into fists. "Those fools!"

> > > > >

Athrun approached the next ship and switched his mobile suit into mobile armor form. He opened the front claws—Scylla multiphase energy canons protruded forth—and a blinding pulse of energy shot from the gun muzzles. The Rowe's fuselage was eviscerated.

From the corner of his eye, Athrun saw the Strike approach. He quickly switched back into mobile suit form and fired both rifles straight at Kira.

> > > > >

La Flaga had already taken out one GINN. He took out another, and then chased the third and final one down. Deploying his gun barrels, the Zero fired a steady stream of bullets. Caught in the hail of firepower, the GINN fled. As it retreated, it sent out a single missile: *Zling*—BOOM!

The force of the blow rocked his mobile armor. "Aw, crap," La Flaga muttered. "That's just great. Now I'm useless!"

> > > > >

Amid the chaos, Flay managed to tiptoe onto the bridge just as La Flaga's radio message came over the loud speakers: "This is Lieutenant Mu La Flaga. The Zero's taken severe damage to the fuselage. Returning to ship."

Captain Murrue looked shocked.

Pal called out, "Missiles firing from the Vesalius. Approaching the Rowe!"

Murrue glared, shouting, "Gottfried number one, align sights! Fire!"

The screens flashed, people shouted, everything was happening so fast. Fear gripped Flay. "Papa!" She ran up to Kuzzey at his station. "Which one is Papa's ship?"

"Flay?!" he said.

"We're in the middle of a battle! Get off the bridge!" Natarle screamed at her.

Sai jumped up and grabbed a hold of her. She struggled. "Let me go! Papa's ship! What's happening to it?"

On the screens, missiles soared into the Rowe. The ship shuddered, and then burst into a fireball. It set off a series of chain-reactions among some of the ships closest to it.

The blood drained from Flay's face.

Captain Copeman came up on the monitor. "Archangel!" he shouted. "Leave at once! That is a direct order!"

"But, sir—" Murrue started to reply, when a squeal broke out behind her.

"Papa!!!" Flay screamed. Behind Captain Copeman stood the Undersecretary Allster. Seeing him, Flay began to cry.

Allster began to lose his composure. "This is lunacy, Captain! If the Archangel leaves us—"

Copeman snapped his fingers at a subordinate officer. "Put Undersecretary Allster in an escape pod. Now!" Returning his attention to the Archangel, the captain said, "Get out of here. Do you understand?" He switched off communications.

"Papa! Papa!" Flay became hysterical as Sai dragged her away.

"Flay, sweetheart," he crooned. "You can't stay here!"

She wrapped her arms around the upper railing, refusing to leave. Eventually Sai overpowered her and pulled her out of the doors. From the bridge, Officer Pal called out, "Two GINNs approaching the Montgomery! They've only got one mobile armor left!" The doors closed.

Flay fell to her knees, tucking in on herself. Sai hung over her back, hugging her. Faintly, she whispered, "Kira."

"What?" Sai asked.

She turned, looking up at him in desperation. "What about Kira? What about him?"

"He-he's fighting hard. But the Aegis is out there too."

"But he said everything would be all right." She fisted his shirt. "He said we would be okay."

"And we are," Sai said softly. "Everything is gonna be fine." He said it over and over as he walked her to her quarters.

Farther down the hallway, they heard the faint sounds of someone singing. The voice was clear, gentle, exquisite. It was completely in contrast with the situation. A dark frown formed on Flay's face. It was that girl—the Coordinator. She sat there, singing, while they were at war! She *mocked* them.

Tearing herself out of Sai's grip, she stalked up to the Coordinator's room and threw open the door.

> > > > >

Natarle watched the monitors, aghast. Their fleet had been decimated by the Coordinators. The final Moebius defender was shot down. Only the Montgomery remained. The Earth Force was cornered and the crew above the Archangel knew it.

"Prepare to fire the Lohengrins!" she shouted. "The GINNs are swooping in. What the hell is the Strike doing?"

La Flaga entered the bridge, looking a little worse for wear. He said, "Don't worry about the kid. Just pull back or we're not gonna make it."

The Strike barely held its own against the Aegis and was in no position to support their battleship. Ever since that girl started freaking out on the bridge, Murrue couldn't figure out what to do. She was still too wet behind the ears to lead decisively and it annoyed Natarle to no end.

The GINN sped up to the Montgomery and hefted its bazooka. It launched a torpedo, the single round knocking out the Montgomery's main gun. Just then, the door to the bridge opened. It was that girl—Flay Allster. Her face was ashen; her eyes, crazed. She dragged Lacus Clyne with her, a gun to the Coordinator's temple. "Tell them that if they shoot Papa's ship, I'll kill her. Tell them!" she screamed. Sai ran in behind her and stopped, speechless. Everyone froze. "Tell them now!"

Natarle liked the way this girl thought. But it was too late. On screen, they saw the Vesalius hurl out its full power from the main gun. Two beams of light shot through space and crippled the Montgomery's fuselage. An explosion cracked its shell, enveloping the ship in a firestorm. Not a single escape pod had been able to launch before the ship imploded.

The screen whited-out and when the glare subsided, only the scattered remains of the ship could be seen hurtling through space. Flay gaped. She started wailing. She dropped the gun, and her hostage, sinking to the floor with sobs. Lacus Clyne and Sai stared at her as she moaned and cried.

The ZAFT vessels now changed course, seeking new prey. And only the Archangel was left. Murrue, of course, sat frozen in her seat. "Captain!" Natarle shouted. But Murrue didn't move. Natarle jumped up and stepped into the upper level, snatching the intercom away from Kuzzey.

"Hailing the ZAFT forces!" she shouted. Murrue looked blankly at her as she continued, "Hailing ZAFT! This is the Earth Alliance ship Archangel! We have custody of Supreme Council Chairman Siegel Clyne's daughter, Lacus Clyne, and we are guarding her aboard this ship. Hold your fire."

> > > > >

Back on the Vesalius, Ades raised his eyebrows. "Miss Lacus?" The girl appeared on their monitors from aboard the Paw.

The broadcast continued: "We discovered her rescue pod and have been guarding her for humanitarian reasons. If you attack this ship, we will consider it an insult to our good will." The woman paused, before coldly declaring, "Furthermore, we will consider it abandonment of Miss Clyne and proceed to act accordingly."

It wasn't hard to read between the lines: attack the Archangel and Lacus would die. Creuset sneered. "They fly to her rescue, and then the tide turns against them . . . suddenly they've got a hostage."

Ades looked over at the commander, waiting for orders. The blond man waved his hand and sighed. "All forces, cease fire."

> > > > >

The mobile suits could hear the broadcast coming from the Archangel over their radios. Kira gasped.

"Cowards!" Athrun spat out. "Holding a civilian girl hostage. Is this your brand of justice, Kira? Are these the friends you've chosen to fight for?"

Kira couldn't open his mouth. It was inexcusable.

The order came: The Aegis and remaining GINN were to return to the ship. Athrun shouted into the intercom, "I'll get her back. I swear it!"

Kira watched the Aegis speed away, ashamed.

> > > > >

Murrue glared at Natarle. She violently switched off the intercom.

"We can't let the Archangel sink," Natarle explained.

"I'm aware of that fact, *Ensign Lieutenant*." Murrue stiffly turned to the screen and watched the Aegis withdraw into the

Vesalius. She knew that Natarle had only acted in their best interests; however, it felt horribly wrong. Only a few hours ago they had descended on the debris of Junius Seven like vultures, and now they were using an innocent girl as a human shield. Was survival worth such dishonor?

The fate of the crew and the refugees rested squarely on her shoulders. Murrue grew frustrated. "We've avoided the crisis only temporarily." The enemy ships had retreated, yes, but the Earth Force fleet had been obliterated. ZAFT would not let up for long.

"At least we've bought a little time to reorganize," Natarle defended. "Let's get done what we need to."

Murrue looked down and sighed. "Yes."

> > > > >

Kira landed the Strike, jumped out of the cockpit, and stomped right up to La Flaga. "What the hell is going on?"

"It's exactly what it looks like," the Hawk of Endymion replied matter-of-factly. "We're trying to stay alive." The older man turned his back on Kira, striding down the corridor to the bridge.

"Don't you mean, we're taking a girl hostage in order to save our necks?" Kira asked, furious. He stalked after the older pilot, whom he'd started to look at as a mentor. "Is the Earth Force an army or a band of thugs?"

La Flaga rounded on him, his face uncharacteristically grim. "You want to know why we did it?" He put his palm on the wall and leaned over Kira. "I'll tell ya, Skinny. It's 'cause we're *weak*.

Kira flinched.

The older pilot had a knack for cutting right to the chase.

La Flaga pushed off the wall and gave Kira some breathing room. "Neither you nor I have the right to criticize the captain or first mate on this. Murrue is just trying to keep us alive."

Kira dropped his gaze and La Flaga walked away. Sighing, he headed toward his quarters to get some rest. Rounding a corner, he heard frantic screams.

"No! Nooooo! Papa! Papaaaaa!"

"Flay," Kira whispered.

He walked slowly toward the commotion in the infirmary. The door was open—he could see Sai, Tolle, and Miriallia trying to console Flay. She looked insane. She shook, screamed, and cried. Snot dripped down her face. Her clothes were disheveled; her hair was a tangled mess. Sai held her as she sobbed.

"It's not true," she yelped. "It can't be true!"

Kira stood in the doorway, horrified. "Flay," he said softly.

She snapped her head up and glared at him with bloodshot eyes. "You . . . *LIAR!*" she roared. Kira stood there as Flay ran up to him and pounded her fists on his chest. "You said it would be okay. It would be all right because *you'd* be out there. Why didn't you protect Papa's ship? Why didn't you help them?"

"Flay!" Kira cried.

Sai tried to silence her, but she broke away from him. "I bet you weren't even fighting seriously. They were all Coordinators, same as you!"

Those words cut deep into Kira's heart.

Flay reached out and grabbed up his shirt, ripping it a bit. "Give me back my father!"

"Flay!" Sai pulled her away. She tore Kira's shirt even further.

"Give me back my father! Give him back! Give him back!"

Kira scrambled backward, shaking his head, running out the door. *They were all Coordinators, same as you.* The Naturals had forced him to fight *because* he was a Coordinator. Now they all thought he was some sort of traitor. His head spun. He didn't acknowledge when Tolle and Miriallia called out to him.

No one could understand his feelings. He'd fought to protect them all; he'd done the best he could. True, he didn't want to kill Athrun. Perhaps if he had, he'd have been able to save the Montgomery. Maybe it *was* his fault that Flay's father had died. Maybe it was fate. Either way, clearly, he could never be one of *them*.

Kira made his way to the zero gravity observation deck to be alone and clear his thoughts. He looked out into deep space—a cry tore from his throat. He banged his fist against the glass wall, pent up rage, fear, and confusion bringing hot tears to his eyes as he held in a sob.

"What's the matter?" asked a sweet voice.

Startled, he turned to see Lacus' innocent expression. She tilted her head, her fingers reaching out to stroke his cheek. Kira blushed and blinked back the moisture in his eyes. He backed away from her touch and sniffed. "What are you doing up here?" he asked.

She smiled faintly. "Taking a walk."

"Look," he said, exasperated, "you can't keep doing this. You can't just get out and walk around whenever you feel like it. They'll think you're a spy."

"But this little pink guy loves walks," she said, pointing to the robo-pet.

"Haro! Haro!"

"Whenever a door is locked, he finds a way to open it," Lacus explained. "He doesn't like being confined."

"Haro! Can't allow it! Haro!" it chirped.

Kira shook his head. Well, at least one riddle was solved: the robo-pet kept letting her out. He watched the girl as she laughed lightly and kicked off the floor, floating up closer to the window. "The fighting is finished, isn't it?"

"For now," Kira replied. "Because of you."

"Me? Oh, yes." She paused, looking at him intensely. "You seem so sad." Her eyes reflected how he felt—but then she smiled and Kira's insides turned to goo.

"I . . . I don't really want to fight, you see." He cleared his throat. "I'm a Coordinator. And Athrun—he's my best friend. So . . ."

"*Athrun?*" she asked suddenly.

Kira told her everything. Every little detail, even the things that had been tucked away, buried deep inside him. He was a student, not a soldier. Athrun was his best friend on the moon, but he had to protect his friends from ZAFT. It was easy to talk to her—she was like him, a Coordinator. And she assumed nothing; she didn't judge him.

Lacus floated over to him when he finished telling his tale. She took his hand and said, "I understand." He could have wept; no one had ever made him feel so accepted and understood. "Both you and Athrun are good people," she murmured. "It's all so sad."

Kira asked in surprise, "You know Athrun?"

"Mm, yes. I'm engaged to marry him." She smiled.

Despite being in zero gravity, Kira felt like the floor had just dropped out from under him.

Lacus laughed, a glint in her eye. "He gave me Haro. He's very kind, you know."

She hugged the pink robo-pet. "When he showed it to me, I told him that I liked it so much, I wanted another one the next time he came to see me. Now, whenever we meet, he brings me another robo-pet."

Kira stared in amazement. He could just imagine Athrun coming to Lacus' house, dozens of Haros in his arms. He could see Lacus accepting them cheerfully, a flock of the silly things chirping all around them. Kira burst out laughing. "Athrun hasn't changed," he said. "He made me a robo-pet, too."

"Really?" Lacus' eyes sparked with interest.

"Yeah. His name's Birdy. He followed some students to the evacuation shelter on Heliopolis and now he's here on this ship. I can show you sometime."

"I'd like that."

Suddenly Kira missed Athrun intensely. The distance between them didn't seem so great, now that they had Lacus binding them together. Going back into battle again would be that much more agonizing.

He shook his head. To take Lacus hostage like this, after she'd been so kind. To wield her like a pawn. "It's no use."

Lacus titled her head.

"Everything feels like a mistake," Kira murmured. But there was one thing he could do to make things right: return Lacus to Athrun. He grasped her hand. "Please, come with me?"

She didn't understand, but she followed him with complete trust. They floated off the observation deck and ran smack-dab into Tolle.

"Hey, buddy. Whatcha up to?"

Kira looked away, suddenly nervous. "Please just let us go, Tolle. I can't take this anymore."

Tolle peered at Kira silently. The moments stretched out. "I guess we're the bad guys this time, stealing the girl away. Maybe you've got plans to steal her back?"

Kira looked up, hopeful.

"I'll help you," Tolle whispered. He led them down the corridor and into the pilots' locker room. Tolle stood guard while Kira took out a spacesuit for Lacus. "Here, put this on."

Kira swept Lacus with his gaze. It was no use—she wore an intricate outfit, complete with a hoopskirt. She saw his confusion and grinned. Taking the dress' straps off her shoulders, she smoothly pulled the bottom half of her skirt off. The remaining top was a miniskirt. Blushing, Kira averted his eyes from her slender legs.

Once they were suited up, they made their way to the empty hangar. Lacus and Kira squeezed into the Strike's cockpit. She waved goodbye to Tolle. "We'll meet again, won't we?"

"Uhm . . . maybe?" Tolle said. His expression turned solemn as he looked at Kira. "You're coming right back, right?"

Kira booted up the OS and then looked down at Tolle. He would *not* cry, dammit.

Officer Murdoch's voice boomed over the intercom. "Hey! What are you kids up to?"

Tolle repeated, "You're coming back, right? Right?!?"

Kira nodded and closed the hatch. A smile lit up his face. How could he think he was all alone, when he had friends like Tolle to help him?

"Promise me, Kira!" Tolle shouted as the engine started up. Alarms sounded; workers and soldiers rushed in.

The Strike walked toward the launch pad. Kira used his outside speaker: "I'm opening the hatch. Everyone better evacuate the hangar!"

With no desire to be yanked into the vacuum of space, the Archangel personnel dashed for the exits. Kira strapped the Aile Striker onto his back, took one last look at Tolle, and crossed his fingers to signal his promise: he'd come back.

> > > > >

Murrue nearly jumped out of the captain's seat when the klaxons blared. "What's going on?" she demanded.

On screen, the Strike bolted from the hangar.

"Kira!" Natarle shouted into the intercom. "What are you doing?"

La Flaga's voice rang out over the system. "The little runt has taken the girl! We can't go in, the airlock's open."

"What?!" Natarle clenched her fists.

Murrue sat among the noise and confusion on the bridge and grinned. "Way to go, kid," she murmured under her breath.

> > > > >

Creuset was taking a hot shower when a summons rang from the bridge. He stepped out and grabbed a towel before switching on the radio. "What is it?"

"Commander! We've confirmed that a mobile suit launched from the Archangel."

Oh? He hadn't seen this coming . . . "I'll be right there," he said. He ran a towel through his long hair and got into a freshly pressed uniform. Going to the desk, he took out a bottle of pills and popped two. He starred down at his trembling hands, willing the pain away, and put on his mask.

Composure carefully in place, he left for the bridge.

> > > > >

Kira switched his radio to all frequencies and spoke into the intercom. "This is the mobile suit Strike of the Earth Alliance Force's Archangel. Miss Lacus Clyne is with me. I'm prepared to hand her over." He paused, forcing himself to take a breath. "I will release her under the following conditions: one, the Nazca-class ship will cease all hostilities; two, the Aegis pilot will meet me alone." He hesitated. "I cannot—and will not—guarantee her safety otherwise."

Lacus didn't even blink; she trusted him not to hurt her. She understood him.

> > > > >

Ades frowned. "What are they up to?"

Athrun popped up on the screen, standing at a communications station in the hangar. "Commander!" he cried. "Please, let me go. I can handle this."

Creuset smoothly responded, "We don't know what the enemy's intentions are, Athrun. Nor whether Miss Lacus is actually on board that Gundam."

"Commander. I'm asking you to trust me."

Creuset smiled gently. "But I do, Athrun. You may go."

"Thank you, sir."

Ades switched off the monitor and turned to the commander. "Are you certain, sir?"

"No." The blond man grinned. "There's always hope. Still, Athrun is quite young and naïve. Stop the ship and prepare my CGUE, just in case."

Knowing better than to question the commander's orders, Ades saw it done.

> > > > >

"Captain!" Natarle said to Murrue. "They're actually doing what he says! This is the perfect time to attack!"

La Flaga buzzed in from the intercom. "You do that, sweet cheeks, and the Strike will turn around and attack *us*. I'm sure of it."

Natarle stood there, speechless. She was a military

officer; such treason simply couldn't be fathomed. The ace pilot grinned at her stupor, winked at Murrue, and switched off the monitor.

Murrue let out a little laugh. Of course, outwardly she had to appear severely displeased, but inwardly, she congratulated Kira's initiative. She watched Natarle work herself up into a frenzy and had to bite her lip to keep from smiling.

Officer Pal said, "The Nazca-class' engines have stopped. The Aegis is approaching the Strike."

She wondered if everything would really go down as Kira had planned.

> > > > >

Athrun approached the Strike slowly, firing his thrusters, hitting the brakes just a few feet from Kira's cockpit. Kira hailed him over the radio.

"Athrun Zala?"

"Yes."

"Open your cockpit."

Athrun opened the hatch. His suit protected him against space, but if the Strike took aim with its beam rifle, he was as good as dead—his body would disintegrate instantly. He knew Kira well enough; there was no deception in the boy's nature. Even though they were enemies, Athrun had faith in him.

Kira opened the Strike's hatch. "Go ahead and say something."

"Huh?" a female murmured.

"He can't see your face," Kira explained to her. "Let him know it's really you."

"Oh!" The slight figure next to Kira waved her hand. "Hello, Athrun. It's been awhile."

That was Lacus, no mistake. Athrun breathed a sigh of relief. "Confirmed," he said.

"You can take her with you," Kira said.

Athrun unbuckled his safety belt, climbed out of his cockpit, and floated up to the Aegis' hatch, bracing himself. Kira gently helped Lacus out of the Strike and pushed her toward Athrun. He caught her, curling her into his arms. They shared a look before turning back to Kira.

"Thanks for everything, Mister Kira," Lacus said softly. Athrun noted the warmth in her voice. No doubt Kira had been kind to her. While Athrun's temper made him prone to mood swings, Kira was shy and sweet and could get along with anyone. Just like Lacus. The two of them probably were so polite to each other it would have given a normal person a toothache.

He missed his friend . . . "Kira!" he shouted. "You can come with us! What reason do you have to be in the Earth Force? Come with me!" The three of them, together—nothing would have given Athrun greater joy.

"I don't want to fight you," Kira said bitterly. "But . . . there are people on that ship that I have to protect! Friends . . ."

Friends.

That single word scalded. Any hopes Athrun had of bringing Kira into the fold were now dashed. If Kira's Natural friends were more important than his brethren, then that was that. "So. It can't be helped." Athrun's voice went cold. "The next time we meet, Kira, it will be to fight."

Kira stared at him for a long time, and then shut the Strike's hatch. Athrun watched as the other boy flew away.

> > > > >

Aboard the Vesalius, Captain Ades reported, "The mobile suit Strike is leaving."

Commander Creuset was already inside his CGUE. He grimaced. "Start the ship's engines, Captain!" he bellowed, launching his machine.

> > > > >

The Archangel quickly detected the enemy. "Mobile suit launched," Officer Pal informed them. "The Nazca-class has started its engines."

Through the Zero's intercom, La Flaga shouted, "I *knew* this was gonna happen!"

"Lieutenant?" Murrue questioned.

Their ace pilot was already suited up and ready to take his mobile armor out. "Captain. Permission to launch?"

Nodding, she said, "Do it."

The Hawk of Endymion wasted no time, rocketing into space. Kira's surprised voice came over the radio. "Lieutenant La Flaga? What are you doing here?"

"Oh, kid, did you think they'd just turn and walk away?"

Kira choked.

"What?"

"You just handed over our safety net. Congratulations, we're back at square one." Strangely enough, La Flaga wasn't the least bit bitter; he actually felt *proud* of Kira. There'd be plenty of time to regret things later, when they were all dead.

> > > > >

Commander Creuset's smooth voice spilled through the Aegis' cockpit. "Bring Miss Lacus back to the ship immediately."

Disheartened, Athrun obeyed. The commander had planned to attack the Naturals from the very beginning. By pretending to accept Kira's conditions, they'd taken advantage of the situation, and now the Strike was a sitting duck. And Athrun couldn't make a move without putting Lacus in danger.

Suddenly Lacus pitched forward, grabbing the intercom microphone. "Commander Rau Le Creuset. Stop this! I am ordering you to stop this at once! Do you truly intend to do battle while I, the memorial service representative for Junius Seven, am in your custody?" Athrun had never seen his fiancée so hard-edged or so . . . mature. "You are to stop your aggressions at once, do you understand me?"

There was a pregnant pause before Creuset's voice patched through. "Understood, Miss Clyne."

Athrun sat there in utter astonishment as Lacus dropped the microphone and smiled sweetly.

> > > > >

Kira watched as the CGUE spun around and returned to the Vesalius. He had no idea why, but they'd somehow managed to avoid a crisis.

"I don't know what happened," La Flaga said over the radio, "but we're not going to stick around to find out. Let's let sleeping dogs lie, huh?"

Reversing the Strike, Kira followed the Zero back toward the hangar. Suddenly La Flaga's wistful voice teased over the intercom, "She was an extraordinary princess, wasn't she, Skinny?"

Blushing, he kept silent. He felt like he'd just let an exotic bird out of its cage.

"What's a-matter, kiddo?"

"N-nothing." He looked down. When Athrun beckoned him, he had wanted to go. He wanted to be with his own kind. But he'd chosen this side—La Flaga's side. Tolle's side. Earth's side.

"Kid?"

Kira swept into the Archangel and shut off the communication system. He didn't want the older pilot to see him sniffling like this.

> > > > >

On the Gamow's bridge, Yzak, Dearka, and Nicol stood at a strategy panel, exchanging ideas. The Vesalius was on its way to return Lacus Clyne to the Lacony Fleet, which left the Gamow to trail after the Archangel.

Nicol looked intently at the ship on the panel. "We can certainly pursue the Paw—I mean, the Archangel—before it joins the moon base, but . . ." He made some quick calculations. "We only have about ten minutes before we enter the moon fleet's firing range."

"Then let's not waste those ten crucial minutes," Yzak said.

Nicol looked away. "The coward's gone quiet," Dearka said.

Yzak ignored them both. "We have ten minutes to make something happen. Or we can sit here and watch our only opportunity get away."

"I second that," Dearka said. "We won't know if our surprise attack works unless we try it, right?"

Nicol stammered, "I know, but—"

Yzak interrupted, "The Vesalius will return home soon. They'll be greeted with the news that we've sunk the Paw." The boy's eyes lit up; he was thirsty for glory. With the Vesalius away, he could finally get out from Athrun's shadow. "Are you with me?"

"Absolutely!" Dearka replied.

Nicol nodded weakly.

> > > > >

Tolle and Miriallia waited outside the interrogation room while Kira got the third degree. Eventually they let him out; he looked a little dazed but otherwise fine. "You okay?" Miriallia asked. "What did they say?"

"Did you get toilet-cleaning duty for a week, too?" Tolle wondered.

La Flaga came out of the room and chuckled, folding his arms. "Hey, Kira, that's not a bad idea." He patted Kira's shoulder and walked off. Natarle came out of the room and gave the boys a cold glare before stalking after La Flaga.

The students slouched a bit as soon as she was out of sight. "I'm okay," Kira said. He looked at Tolle. "Toilet cleaning, huh?"

"Tolle got chewed out by Officer Murdoch for letting you leave." Miriallia snickered. "As punishment, he has to clean the latrines for a week."

"With a toothbrush," Tolle added mournfully. "At any rate, we'll be joining up with the moon fleet soon. I can take it until then."

Kira laughed, hooking an arm around Tolle's shoulders. "Oh man, I'm sorry! Hey, I'll help you out, of course." They made their way down the corridor.

"To tell you the truth, I was kinda worried." Tolle licked his lips. "Your friend . . . the Aegis pilot. I'm sorry . . . I overheard you talking to Lacus."

Kira tripped a little. Tolle heard everything he said? What would his friends think of him now?

Tolle smiled. "I'm glad you came back." He spoke genuinely and it touched Kira's heart. He'd made the right decision. For the first time in a long time, Kira felt good.

They left, unaware that Flay was hiding just around the corner, listening in. Her hair was a mess. Her eyes had a vacant look. She murmured hoarsely, "I won't let things stand like this, Kira Yamato."

> > > > >

"It's been a long haul," Sai said to Kuzzey, "but only a little further to go." They sat in the mess hall, finally able to eat in peace. The Archangel would soon join the moon fleet. It would all seem like a bad dream once they landed. The students would be reunited with the rest of the refugees from Heliopolis and then take shuttles to Earth.

"Maybe we'll be able to go to Earth right after reaching the moon. I'm tired of all this military stuff," Kuzzey said.

Sai shrugged. "Didn't Captain Ramius say something about having to wait until we make contact?"

"Yeah. But if the moon fleet is expecting us, it shouldn't take too long, right? So, what do you think is gonna happen to Kira?" Kuzzey asked solemnly. They'd always taken for granted that Kira was one of them. But the fact that he was a Coordinator . . . and the only one who could pilot the Strike . . . Would the Earth Alliance really just let him go?

Kira entered the mess hall and Sai and Kuzzey quickly looked away. Too late—it was obvious they'd been talking about him. Kira got some water, trying not to make things more awkward.

Just then, Flay wandered in. Sai got up and said, "Flay? You okay? You should be resting." She didn't even look at him, but instead went straight to Kira. He stepped back but Flay just stood there, her head hung low.

"Kira . . ." she said quietly. "I'm so sorry about everything."

"Huh?" Kira said.

"I–I panicked. And I said and did some terrible things." Tears spilled over onto her pale cheeks. "Please forgive me? I know . . . I know you're fighting hard to protect all of us. I just—"

"Flay," Kira said softly. "It's all right. Put it out of your mind."

She shook her head. "I knew it, too! I knew you were out there, fighting for us, but still I . . . I . . ."

Kira's lips curved into a smile, bit by bit. He looked on her with compassion. "Thanks, Flay. I'm sorry that I . . . I wasn't able to protect your father." He bowed, at a loss for words.

"I hate war," she spat out. "I hope it's over soon."

Their conversation was cut short by the ship's alarms signaling Level One battle deployment. Kira put down his cup and looked at his friends. Flay tensed. "We were ready to rendezvous! Almost!"

Everyone hurried out of the mess hall and into the corridor. A small girl, a Heliopolis refugee, got lost in the confusion. She tripped right into Kira and landed on her bottom.

"Sorry!" Kira cried, putting his hands out to pick her up. "Are you okay?"

Flay stepped in front of him and kindly picked the girl up. "He's in a big hurry," she said to the child. "It's the war again. But we'll be okay. He's out there to protect us."

"Rweally?" the girl asked, looking timidly at Kira.

"Really," Flay assured. "Don't you worry. He'll take care of the bad guys."

"Kira!" Sai called up ahead. Kira smiled at the little girl and ran off. He looked back over his shoulder; Flay and the child were holding hands.

"That's right," Flay muttered. "He'll beat them." She squeezed her hands tightly and the little girl cried out in pain. Flay didn't even look at her. A cold smile split her mouth. The child was frightened by the wicked glare and ran away. Flay just stood there and repeated in an eerie tone, "All of them. He'll beat all of them."

> > > > >

From the bridge, Miriallia quickly radioed the Strike and told Kira of the situation. "ZAFT has one Laurasia-class and three mobile suits: the Duel, the Buster, and the Blitz." She checked her readings. "Strike, stand by. All systems go. Strike, you are clear to launch!"

As Kira jettisoned from the Archangel, Murrue announced, "The moon fleet is on its way. Hang on!" Their enemy would never stop chasing them, she knew, but she absolutely would not let this ship sink. "Move the Igelstellung and prepare anti-beam depth charges!" she ordered. "Ready all stern missiles!"

The three mobile suits came at them in close formation. Suddenly, the ships scattered. A white line of fire shot from the Gamow. "Evasive action!" Murrue shouted. The Archangel dodged the first volley but took the next hit. The hull shook violently. Murrue groaned, straining to keep her seat and her composure.

They did have a strategy, after all: La Flaga's Zero would take on the Buster, Kira's Strike would challenge the Duel, and the Archangel would be left alone to take on the Blitz. As the mobile suits pressed in, Murrue shouted, "Valiant fire!"

The enemies easily dodged the attack and then, suddenly, the Blitz disappeared within a haze of heat. Bewildered, Tonomura said, "I've lost the Blitz! It must have deployed the Mirage Colloid."

Murrue ordered, "Fire anti-beam depth charges. Ready anti-air shrapnel!"

The depth charges shot out and dispersed. The Archangel tracked the sea of scattered charges with an illumination beam. "Estimate the Blitz's position from the beam angle," Murrue said.

Once the Blitz's approximate location was calculated and the data streamed into the stern missile's computers, Natarle barked, "Fire anti-air shrapnel!"

The missiles split into dozens of warheads. The mobile suit's Phase Shift armor switched on and the Mirage Colloid faded away. To keep the Gundam from disappearing again, the Archangel's Igelstellung fired continuously.

The Blitz retreated, unable to use its invisibility defense. It was only a temporary respite, however—it returned with its full armor activated, wielding its powerful beam rifle.

> > > > >

Kira growled as he fired his beam rifle at the Duel. The enemy blocked with its shield—deflected beam particles burst between them like fireworks. He could see La Flaga's Zero zipping past, firing its gun barrels at the Buster.

The Gamow's main gun blasted out again, scoring a direct hit on the Archangel. Miriallia's voice scratched through the waves of electronic interference. "Ki—Return—ship! We—hit!"

Narrowly avoiding the Duel's saber, Kira turned to see the Archangel, burning.

The Blitz strafed the Archangel at point-blank range. The ship's armor overheated, glowing white-hot.

Don't worry. He'll take care of the bad guys. Kira remembered what Flay said to the little girl aboard the Archangel. All his friends . . . the refugees . . . He wouldn't let them sink!

He saw the Duel's saber swing down in slow motion—*Zling!* His focus sharpened; he was able to perceive several things simultaneously. He swung his own saber up, sliced the Duel's side, (sparks shot out like blood) and then ignited his thrusters and did a fast burn toward the Archangel.

It was weird, but he *sensed* the Duel following him. Its beam rifle fired—he dodged nimbly, dead-set on the Blitz. He honed in on the mobile suit and fired relentlessly at the

Archangel's attacker. The Blitz tried to spring back, but Kira was faster. The Strike kneed the Blitz in the torso.

The Duel brandished its saber and sprung its Armor Schneider blades from its hips. Kira switched monitors and grasped the daggers jutting out from the Duel faster than the human eye could perceive. The blades had barely ejected before Kira grabbed them and thrust both into the Duel's punctured armor. Sparks jetted as Kira scraped the daggers down the Duel's fuselage. It was a mortal blow. The Duel froze.

The Blitz rushed forward and carried the Duel out of range, sweeping the damaged Gundam away like a powerful tide. Meanwhile, Kira stood before the Archangel like a guard dog, sighing and closing his eyes.

"They're running away! Well done, kiddo!" La Flaga said, beaming as he popped on the monitor. Kira felt like he was waking from an ether-induced dream.

"Huh?"

"Skinny . . . you . . ." La Flaga's eyes looked a little misty.

"What?" Kira asked breathlessly.

"Nothing, kid. I'm just saying—you're amazing! That's all."

Kira blushed at the compliment.

> > > > >

Nicol radioed from the Blitz, "Dearka! Withdraw! The enemy fleet is on its way!"

Those ten precious minutes had long since been up.

"Dammit!" Dearka cursed.

The Archangel had remarkable armor and held up better than anyone could have predicted. It found a way around the Blitz's Mirage Colloid with the shrapnel volleys. And the Strike . . . Such mobility and reaction speed—Natural or Coordinator, that was no ordinary pilot.

"Yzak? Are you all right? Yzak?" Dearka called.

The only sounds coming from the Duel were groans, followed by a furious whisper, "It hurts . . . it hurts . . ." as Nicol rushed them toward the Gamow.

> > > > >

Athrun approached Lacus' door and tapped the intercom switch. "Hello. I came to visit with you."

The door opened and a lump of pink bounded at him. "Haro! Haro! Athrun! Athrun!"

Flustered, he caught Haro in mid-flight.

Lacus laughed. "Haro's in good spirits. He seems happy to see you, Athrun."

"I don't think he has emotions," he said despondently. Every time he saw Lacus smile like that, so innocently, he felt small. Dirty. It had been such a long time since they'd last been together. Now it was awkward.

"Athrun?" She looked worried.

"Yeah. Ahem. How are you? I mean . . . after being taken hostage and all."

She shrugged. "I'm fine. Your friend on the ship took good care of me."

Of course he did. "I see." He tried to hide the bitterness from his voice, but he just couldn't.

Lacus smiled sadly. "Kira is a very nice person. Strong."

"He's a moron!" Athrun blurted out. "He's not even a soldier, but he's piloting that thing! He's being used by the Earth Force and he knows it!" He shook. "Even if you say he's my friend, both his parents were Naturals, so—"

Lacus' hand smoothed through his hair. She spoke seriously, "He told me he doesn't want to fight you anymore."

Athrun's anger deflated. "I feel the same way! Who would, with him?"

Lacus looked up at him with those mesmerizing eyes. She touched his cheek but he pulled back. He'd never been this open with his fiancée—he was ashamed at the unbridled emotion he'd displayed. Calming himself, he switched to a neutral tone. "The Lacony Fleet is waiting. We should go to the launch pad."

He headed for the door when she said, "You look so bitter, Athrun."

"What sort of monster smiles while waging war, Lacus?" he asked simply.

> > > > >

Inside the Vesalius' hangar, Creuset and the pilots waited to see Lacus Clyne off. The commander was not amused by her prior interference, but he hid it well behind his mask.

Lacus respectfully nodded at him and said, "Commander Creuset, thank you for everything."

He saluted with a smile. "The Lacony Fleet will take responsibility for your safety and see you home."

"Will the Vesalius return for the Memorial Service?" she inquired.

"That's hard to say," he hedged. How typical. They had a war to win and this girl was concerned with such a waste of time . . . Still, he had to remain diplomatic. "I suppose battles are important, but we must never forget their victims."

"I'll take that to heart," she said dryly, gazing at him with sharp eyes. He smiled thinly. "I'll see you again," she said with a chill in her voice.

Diplomacy be damned; this was old-fashioned sparring. How surprising that Athrun's little fiancée had a spine of steel. Creuset reminded himself not to underestimate her.

"War is so complicated," she said to Athrun. "Why must you fight?" Athrun made no reply and Creuset squashed the urge to roll his eyes. Suddenly, she smiled. "I look forward to seeing you again, Athrun."

Creuset watched as Lacus kissed Athrun on the cheek—
the boy looked like he would faint—and then she boarded her
ship and the hatch closed. As soon as the shuttle departed,
Creuset *did* roll his eyes, draping an arm around Athrun.

The Earth Alliance Force's moon fleet slowly approached the Archangel. It looked like an armada of toy ships on a lake of glass. Sunlight reflected off the port side. The flagship Menelaos led the fleet to surround the Archangel, enclosing it in an array of battleships and destroyers.

On the bridge, Murrue gave orders to match the Menelaos' speed. Admiral Halberton had personally set their navigation route in order to get close enough for a good look at the new battleship. More than anyone else in the Atlantic Federation, Admiral Halberton had backed the development of the X Numbers and the Archangel unwaveringly. He believed that they would turn the tide of the war and Murrue heartily agreed. She respected her commanding officer very, very much, and looked on him almost as a mentor.

The ship entered basic inertial navigation and so Murrue left the bridge. "Hold down the fort," she said to Tonomura. "I'll be right back."

Natarle followed her out as they made their way into the elevator. As soon as the door shut, Natarle asked, "What do you intend to do about the Strike?"

"Do?" Murrue blinked.

Impatient, Natarle said, "Everybody on this ship knows that the only reason we made it this far was because of that boy's abilities. He's the only one that could pilot that mobile suit. Are you really going to let him go?"

Murrue frowned; a few days ago, Natarle hated the very notion of a Coordinator simply setting eyes on their prized weapon. Now, she couldn't wait to shove the kid back in the pilot's seat. Fear, Murrue decided, made people ugly.

"I understand your point," she said, "but the fact remains that Kira Yamato is not a soldier in this army."

"But his abilities are too valuable to let him just slip away."

"The Atlantic Federation can't draft an Orb citizen just because of his abilities. You realize this, right?" Murrue said wryly.

Natarle snapped her mouth shut with an audible click and they rode the rest of the way in silence.

> > > > >

"I don't see what all the fuss is about. We've already met up with the fleet," Kira said, poking his head into the Zero's hatch. Inside the hangar bay, mechanics scrambled to get the Moebius back in perfect working order.

La Flaga smiled up at Kira from the cockpit. "If it's anything less than one-hundred percent, I can't relax. And if *I* can't relax, *you* can't relax." He winked.

Kira was really looking forward to taking a break after their rendezvous. Instead, he worked harder than ever helping to make repairs on the Zero and prepare the Gundam. It seemed silly; who in their right mind would attack a fleet of this size? Along with too many battleships to count, there were dozens of mobile armors ready for deployment. They were safe.

But La Flaga wouldn't relax. When Kira asked Officer Murdoch about it, the scruffy man just laughed. "The moon fleet might be big, but their pilots are all amateurs. If anything happened out there, they'd come crying to us, relying on the Hawk again."

Kira glanced at the Zero. La Flaga was definitely an original. Even though Kira's Coordinator abilities made him fast and accurate, he had his hands full going up against one Gundam at a time. La Flaga, however, had taken out several GINNs and immobilized the Buster, using only a damaged mobile armor.

The older man came out of the Moebius and wiped his hands on his shirt. Kira looked away, a little embarrassed to be caught gawking. He wondered what would happen to the Strike's OS now. Kira had specifically tailored it for himself. "What about the Strike?" he asked La Flaga. "Will it be okay to leave the OS like it is?"

La Flaga looked puzzled. "I know what you mean, but if we changed it back, it would lower all the specs."

"Well, then," Murrue chimed in from the upper deck, "we'll just have to find ourselves a pilot who can operate it as it is."

Everyone craned their necks to see her walk across the catwalk and jump down onto the hangar floor.

La Flaga chuckled. "What are you doing down here? Got a sudden urge to get your hands dirty?"

She smiled at him and then looked at Kira. "Can I borrow him for a minute, Lieutenant?"

Kira swallowed. La Flaga patted him on the back. "Go right ahead. Just be sure and return him when you're all done."

Murrue smiled and said, "No worries. Come on, I just want to chat." They weaved past the maintenance crew and headed toward the corridor that would take Murrue back to the bridge.

"With all that's gone on, I haven't had a chance to talk with you until now."

"Uh huh." Kira said warily.

"I wanted to thank you properly, for once."

"Huh?"

Murrue put a hand on his shoulder. "We forced you to march into hell and you rose to the challenge. People might not say it, but everyone is grateful. Thank you, Kira."

He'd never expected anything like this. "No . . . ugh. It's all right, Captain."

"I'm just worried you might find yourself in a jam on Earth." She squeezed his shoulder. "Stay strong, okay?"

He nodded, completely taken aback.

The crew assembled on the dock as a small white shuttle entered the Archangel's hangar. An older man with a muscular physique, glittering eyes, and a bushy mustache walked down the platform, escorted by armed guards. It was Admiral Halberton. Everyone saluted in unison as he approached the dock.

He stood before Murrue and spoke kindly, "When we received the news that Heliopolis had been destroyed, we thought all hope was lost. I never dreamed you'd make it here. Well done."

"Thank you, Admiral." Murrue breathed. "It's been quite an adventure."

Halberton moved on to La Flaga, returning his salute.

"Mu La Flaga of the Seventh Mobile Fleet, sir," La Flaga fired off.

"Lucky thing you happened to be there, La Flaga," said the Admiral.

The ace pilot cracked a grin. "You can keep that kind of luck, sir."

Halberton made his way down the line of officers, nodding to each one. Afterward, Murrue introduced him to the students who had helped on the bridge. Kira and his friends straightened up as Halberton approached. "These are some refugees from Heliopolis," she said. "Their assistance has been vital to our survival."

The admiral looked on them warmly. "I'm happy to report that we've confirmed that your parents are all safe, ladies and gentlemen." Everyone brightened with the fantastic news. "You served gallantly under extreme circumstances. I thank you and look forward to talking more with you later."

As Halberton left with Murrue and the other officers, the knot in Kira's stomach began to unwind.

Captain Ades checked a transmission. Without looking up, he said to Commander Creuset, "The Ziegler and the Gamow have rendezvoused."

He could care less about Lacus Clyne. "We haven't been spotted by the Naturals?" the Commander asked. He couldn't be sure.

"Our position should be fine; the fleet has withdrawn considerably."

Creuset stroked his jaw. He sighed. "I thought they would head for the moon base now. Looks like they are going to land on Earth after all."

Ades shifted. "Do you suppose they're headed for Alaska?"

Alaska was the Earth Alliance's headquarters. The Archangel would most likely proceed directly to the Supreme Command on the Yukon Delta. ZAFT would never reach them if they made it that far.

"I want to sink her while she's within our grasp," Creuset murmured. "But how?"

"The Ziegler has six GINNs and we have five mobile suits; among them is the Aegis," Ades said. "The Gamow can sortie out the Buster and Blitz."

Staring out into the distance, Creuset made some quick calculations. A cold smile crept upon his face. "Admiral Halberton . . . How can we get him to leave . . . quickly?"

> > > > >

The Admiral sat at a large wooden desk in the captain's room aboard the Archangel. Murrue, Natarle, and La Flaga stood at attention in front of the desk. Halberton's staff officer, Captain Hoffman, was also there. Hoffman said bitterly, "To think this ship and the Strike allowed both Heliopolis and Artemis to be destroyed." He shook his head in disapproval.

Murrue looked straight ahead, her posture erect. Halberton came to her defense, saying, "It is the Earth Force's saving grace that both new weapons did not fall into enemy hands."

Hoffman responded briskly, "It seems Alaska does not agree."

"Humph!" Halberton snorted. "What do *they* know of space warfare? It's easy for those fops to criticize. Lieutenant Ramius knew my wishes and she delivered both vessels to us with nothing more at her disposal than sheer ingenuity. There is no room for complaint."

The tightness in Murrue's chest dissipated somewhat. This praise was a reward in and of itself.

Hoffman changed the subject, but his tone remained bitter. "What about this Coordinator child? Ingenuity or not, this is a sticky situation we've gotten ourselves into."

Murrue wondered at the way the Admiral let his adjutant speak to him. She narrowed her eyes and said sharply, "Kira Yamato wanted to protect his friends. He piloted the Strike with no other thought in mind. Without his abilities, we'd be dead right now. It was traumatic for him to fight his own kind, but he did it bravely, and with absolute selflessness. He is a kind, honest boy. He's more than earned our trust."

Beside her, La Flaga puffed up his chest. She could feel his silent support.

"But to just let him go like this . . ." Natarle said, suddenly taking a step forward. "It may be presumptuous of me, but I agree with Captain Hoffman." La Flaga and Murrue stared at her, but she ignored them and continued, "His abilities are truly remarkable. Now that he's discovered the G Weapon, letting him go would not only be a waste, but a threat to our security."

Admiral Halberton smiled. "ZAFT already has four of those machines. The G Weapons aren't exactly a secret any longer."

Natarle wavered for a moment, then burst out, "But his abilities—if it's possible, they should remain at the army's disposal!"

"But what if he doesn't want to join the army?" Halberton steepled his hands. "We can't just draft an Orb citizen."

"Both of his parents are Naturals. They escaped the destruction of Heliopolis and are now on Earth," Natarle said. "If we could bring them in for our *protection* . . . perhaps he could be persuaded."

Murrue felt ill. This scheme was truly disgusting. Using a boy's parents as leverage to force him into service? Such a thing ought to be beneath them. Natarle's blind loyalty to the army and her own ambition sickened Murrue. She would not use Kira like a pawn.

Halberton slammed his palm down on the desk and thundered, "Don't even suggest such a preposterous idea! What *use* would a coerced soldier be?" He dropped his mask of manners and instantly morphed into an icon of indignant authority.

Natarle startled. "I–I'm sorry, sir."

The admiral stood up and said with an icy glare, "Enough. Focus on what lies ahead." He turned and smiled at Murrue. "From here on out, the Archangel will depart for Alaska. Maintain your current crew."

Murrue held her breath as Captain Hoffman said, "There's nothing else we can do. The Eighth Fleet's vanguard and supplement crew are gone. We have no additional personnel to spare for the Archangel."

"All our research on the X Numbers was lost on Heliopolis," Halberton said. "It's vital that you get the Archangel and that Gundam back to Alaska."

"But we don't have the staff," she said. With Kira and the students leaving, they were down to a skeletal crew. There was no way they'd make it.

Hoffman spoke plainly. "We'll escort you to the orbit separation point. From there, you will descend directly to headquarters." He smiled at her. "We must continue developing the Gundams. ZAFT is throwing new machines into the pot, one after another, while our bureaucrats keep shoveling money into useless pet projects. Their only experience with battle is making casualty lists."

Murrue completely understood Halberton's outrage. She had seen first-hand the terrible reality of battleships and mobile armors engaging the enemy's mobile suits. Saluting, she said, "Understood, Admiral."

Captain Hoffman sniffed sullenly. The difference between Hoffman, a paper-pusher, and Halberton, a seasoned veteran, only illustrated the dissimilarities between their headquarters and the frontlines. Murrue knew that she'd run into a lot more of Hoffman's ilk on Earth and that it would take a great deal of convincing to make Alaska see the desperate reality of their situation in space.

"In accordance with your wishes, and on behalf of the Archangel crew," Murrue said, "we accept the mission to Alaska."

La Flaga saluted as she did. "As the only armor pilot left, I guess I can hardly refuse, huh, sir?"

Halberton blinked at their wayward pilot. Murrue gave a little half-smile as the Admiral solemnly wished them good luck.

In the mess hall, Natarle walked up to the students' table and handed each of them a document. Hoffman stood by as Natarle impatiently called Kira's name. He was nowhere to be found. "Fine," Natarle bit out. "Give this to Kira when you see him," she said, thrusting several more documents at Tolle.

He looked at them. "Military discharge papers?"

Hoffman explained, "Even in emergencies, it's against regulations for civilians to perform combat duties. To avoid criminal procedures, we had you all backdated as enlisted volunteers. *Don't* lose those papers." The severe man cleared his throat. "Now that you've been dismissed, I cannot emphasize enough that what you learned while in service must stay completely confidential."

Flay listened intently, nodding as Hoffman spoke. Natarle said to her, "You weren't fighting. You don't have to worry about it."

"No," Flay replied. She stood up. "I want to enlist in the army," she said resolutely.

Everyone was floored. This petite girl, this little princess, would be totally out of place in the army. The way she had acted on the bridge during a skirmish . . .

"That's ridiculous," Natarle said.

"I mean it!" Flay asserted. "Ever since my father was killed, I've thought a lot about it."

"Ah," Captain Hoffman said, nodding. "You are Undersecretary Allster's daughter."

Flay clenched her fists. "I was in shock when my father was killed. I hated this ship—I wanted out of here. It's all I could think about. But when I learned that we'd be going to Earth it seemed . . . wrong."

"Wrong?" Natarle pressed.

"You'd think I'd feel better, wouldn't you? That I'd be happy to be safe. But it's just the opposite." She shook her head, tears welling up. "There's still a war. It never made any difference to me before. But my father gave his life trying to end it . . ."

Everyone fell silent. "If real peace—and real peace of mind—can only be achieved by getting our hands dirty," Flay said, "then that's what I'll do. I'll carry on my father's work, even though my own contribution may be small." She covered her face and quietly cried.

Sai hugged her, whispering her name gently. He dried her tears and walked her out of the room. Hoffman and Natarle followed them out.

Tolle ran after them. "Sai!"

"I feel the same way as Flay," Sai said over his shoulder. "Anyway, I can't just leave her behind."

Tolle looked down at his discharge papers. He tore them up. "The Archangel is short on staff. I'm not leaving until it's landed."

Miriallia came up behind them. Without hesitation, she ripped her papers in two. "Don't think you're getting away from me that easy, mister."

Kuzzey nodded, joining them. "Well, I guess I can't be left out of all the fun!" He sighed, tearing up his papers too. The torn scraps landed in a heap at their feet. Only one discharge paper was left—Kira's.

> > > > >

Kira had changed into civilian clothes. He walked to the hangar and floated up to the Strike, taking one last look.

"Do you think you'll regret it?" a voice said behind him. "If you leave?" Admiral Halberton stood on the catwalk beside the Gundam. "Kira Yamato, right? I've read your report. I'm astonished. Even by Coordinator standards, your abilities are nothing short of miraculous."

Kira stiffened.

Halberton nodded to the Strike. "We created these to match the ZAFT GINNs. A twist of fate landed you in this one and it turns into the fiercest weapon we have."

He didn't know what to say.

"Your parents are Naturals, aren't they?" the admiral asked.

"Huh? Oh. Yes." Kira nodded.

Halberton peered wistfully at the Strike. "What dreams do you suppose they had for you, making you a Coordinator? What future did they envision for you, I wonder? I want to end this war as quickly as possible," Halberton said. "That's my dream."

An escort officer approached the catwalk. "Sir, the Menelaos is urgently requesting your return."

"It would seem I'm out of time," the admiral said, shrugging. "Thank you for protecting the Archangel, Kira. I'm certain your future will be a very bright one."

The man turned to leave. Kira called out, "Um! The Archangel . . . and Lieutenant Ramius . . . From here on out, what . . .?"

"The Archangel will descend to Earth with its original crew. Then back onto the field they go."

Kira knew that Murrue and the others were soldiers and it was their job to man the battleships, but what hope did they have without the Strike? La Flaga was an amazing pilot, but he couldn't fight the entire war with one mobile armor. At that moment, Kira realized just how deeply he'd become attached to these people, to this ship . . .

Halberton smiled kindly at him. "I can tell by that look on your face that you're worried about them. Kira, your abilities *are* unique. But you alone cannot win this war for us."

He thought about La Flaga, out there on his own. "It can't be coincidence that I ended up here. Maybe piloting the Strike is what I was born to do."

Calmly, Halberton replied, "That's solely up to you. We can't force you to take any actions against your will; the choice is yours." He gazed at Kira for a long time before continuing to the bridge.

> > > > >

When they received the news from the Menelaos that a ZAFT ship had arrived, the Archangel immediately started tracking its movements. Officer Pal reported the readings as they came. "One Nazca-class and two Laurasia-class ships approaching. Estimated arrival in fifteen minutes."

Murrue looked anxiously at the monitor. Did they truly intend to attack the entire fleet simply to get the Archangel?

"It's Creuset," La Flaga said with certainty.

"How do you know?"

"I *know*, Murrue."

She shivered. This commander was fanatical—always waiting for them in the shadows. Her throat constricted. La Flaga shot her a look and she pulled herself together. "Cease landing preparations. Seal the bay! Where is the Menelaos' shuttle? All hands, battle stations Number One!"

> > > > >

Kira went to the landing deck; it was in chaos. The Heliopolis refugees were supposed to transfer to the Menelaos and then take a ship to Earth. The landing crew hauled equipment from the shuttle while the refugees scrambled to board. Kira couldn't spot his friends in the commotion. They wouldn't have boarded without him . . .

Officer Murdoch's scruffy voice boomed, "They sent us Sky Grapplers?" Battle plates for Earth's atmosphere were being removed from the shuttle. Would the Hawk of Endymion use one of those?

"Hello!" said the small girl Kira had bumped into before. She jumped up and floated awkwardly toward him. He pulled her to him protectively. She giggled.

"Thish is for you," she lisped, holding up a paper flower.

"For me?" he asked.

"Yesh. Thanksh for helping ush!"

Smiling, he accepted her gift and gently pushed her toward her mother. They boarded the shuttle. He stared down at the flower. Suddenly he was grappled in a familiar headlock. "Wah, Tolle! Cut it out, man!" Laughing, he looked over his shoulder—to see Tolle in a military uniform. His friend thrust a paper at him.

"Here. It's your military discharge."

Kira blinked.

Sai walked up, rubbing the back of his neck. "We've decided to stay, you see."

"Stay?"

"On the Archangel. With the army."

He reeled. "What are you talking about? Why?"

"It's kinda a long story," Sai replied. "But when you get right down to it, Flay actually volunteered first. One after the other, we all joined up."

Astonished, Kira frowned. Flay? A soldier?

Just then, Murrue's voice came over the speakers. "All hands, battle stations Number One!" Soldiers and staff dropped what they were doing and scrambled to make preparations for battle.

A shuttle guard called to Kira, "Hey, you! We're leaving right now! Are you coming?"

Tolle pushed Kira forward. "Hold on! He's going, he's going!" Tolle latched onto Kira's shoulders, doing a poor job trying to look happy. "It's fate, buddy! You just worry about getting to Earth safely, you hear?"

His friends shouted their goodbyes. Kuzzey looked back over his shoulder. "Whatever you do, Kira, just don't join ZAFT, okay?" They waved and ran toward the bridge.

Kira stood stock still, confused. He was being left behind . . . He was running away . . . Who else would they get to pilot the Strike? What would happen when they engaged the Aegis? If he left now, he'd probably never see Athrun again. In one hand he had his discharge papers—his ticket to freedom. In the other hand, a paper flower. He closed his eyes and clenched his fists.

"Hurry up! Let's go!" the shuttle crewman shouted.

Here was the crux—he could leave now and never have to fight another Coordinator again. Or he could protect the ones he loved. "Go on!" he said. "I'm staying." Kira crumpled the discharge paper and let it float away. Sheltering the paper flower in the palm of his hand, he ran through the launch deck.

> > > > >

The following announcement blared through the Gamow's speakers: "Seal all bulkheads. Three minutes before mobile suit launch. All hands report to your posts!"

Yzak leapt from the infirmary doors. Half his face swathed in bandages, he looked haggard and in pain. A medic followed after him. "You mustn't be up! You need to rest!"

"Shut up! Let go of me!" He shook off the medic's hold and ran feverishly toward the mobile suit hangar bay. The wounds on his face throbbed, but it was nothing compared to his psychological scars. When the Strike had dealt a blow to the Duel's electrical systems, it caused a small-scale explosion in the cockpit. The blast flew directly into Yzak's helmet, singeing his flesh and puncturing half his face with tiny shards from his visor. Had the cockpit itself been cracked, he would have died immediately. Like it or not, he'd survived.

It tormented him that he couldn't dispatch one Natural soldier. It'd ruined his reputation as an ace pilot and he'd sworn revenge. Up until recently, he'd always been confident in his abilities, scoring numerous achievements in battle before. His previous failures to capture the Strike he'd been able to blame on Athrun. But Athrun wasn't there last time. The Strike had taken on the Blitz and the Duel simultaneously and nearly destroyed them both. It was unthinkable, an insult worse than death.

Yzak changed into his pilot suit and boarded the Duel. It was already repaired, outfitted with additional equipment from GINNs that surrounded his entire fuselage. Shoulders, arms, chest, hips, and eyes were covered—he was literally armed to the teeth. His mobile suit was equipped with an Assault Shroud that would strengthen the Duel's firepower and propulsion. On its right shoulder hung a Shiva gun; on the left, a missile pod.

From the bridge, a control officer beamed onto his monitor. "Stop it, Yzak! You're still too—"

"Just do your damned job!" Yzak screamed, advancing the Duel toward the launch pad.

Creuset's smooth voice hailed all three mobile suits over the intercom. "Gentlemen, your target remains the Archangel. Do not waste time on anything else."

Yzak had no intention of wasting time. But he also had no intention of obeying the commander's orders.

> > > > >

The mobile suits sprang from the ZAFT ships—Earth Alliance Moebiuses answered from destroyers and battleships. Admiral Halberton's message issued from the Menelaos: "All ships, take interceptive posture in dense formation. Guard the Archangel!"

Everyone on the Archangel watched their monitors intently. The enemy had three mobile suits and seven GINN coming from three battleships. Yes, the moon fleet was big, but the Nazca-class Vesalius had been able to take out the battleship Montgomery and half the Eighth Fleet all by itself.

Natarle ordered one weapons system into operation after the other. She brought out the Igelstellung, the Corinthos, the Gottfried, and the Lohengrin. Tonomura had his hands full coordinating all that. Their small crew was stretched to the limit and they hadn't even started the descent to Alaska.

"Sorry we're late," Tolle said. The bridge door opened wide as the Heliopolis students clamored on deck. Murrue and the others spun around.

"You came back," Murrue said in utter surprise.

"Say hello to our new volunteers," Natarle explained with a smile. "Captain Hoffman acknowledged them and I approved."

Murrue smiled back.

"Kira's gone," said Sai from the CIC. "We can't take his place, but we're better than nothing, right?"

Tolle waved to Neumann in the pilot's seat. He sighed with relief. The crew was very happy to have the students back. Murrue was glad, but she worried that their selfless actions today might scar them tomorrow.

Kira ran to the pilot's locker room, stopping short when he saw someone holding his uniform. It wasn't La Flaga: too short. "F-Flay?"

She turned sharply. "Kira?" In an instant, she flew into his arms.

He swallowed as she embraced him. "Why-why are you . . .?"

"I thought you'd gone." She clung to him, smiling softly. His heart pounded as she explained, "Everyone's staying to fight. I was the first to do it, but I didn't think they'd stay too. I just want to . . ." She indicated his uniform.

"No!" he said, grasping her shoulders. "You can't pilot the Strike. It would never work."

What had he done? How could he *think* of leaving? How could he let the situation get so bad that one small girl intended to throw her life away like that?

Kira smiled. "It's okay now. I'm back. I'll pilot the Strike for—" He was about to say for her, but thought better of it. "We'll talk after the battle, all right? I won't run away anymore. I've made up my mind now."

Flay sidled close to him. "If so, then . . ." She brushed her lips over his. Kira felt intoxicated—her breath on his lips; her scent; her hair, soft against his face. "My thoughts will be with you. To protect you," she whispered in his ear.

> > > > >

Gunfire burst forth like blossoming flowers as the Moebiuses and the GINNs opened up on each other. The Moebiuses had trouble dodging missiles as the GINNs unloaded their bazookas. Through the haze, the Aegis dove in and out.

The red mobile suit transformed into mobile armor and fired its Scylla from between its claws. Three Moebiuses immediately went down in flames. The Buster and the Duel shot down mobile armors one after another, their mobility and overwhelming firepower unmatched. They set their sights at the heart of the fleet—the Archangel.

Admiral Halberton cursed on the bridge of the Menelaos. "Damn. It's the X Numbers."

Hoffman stood beside him. "They certainly are splendid in battle," he said begrudgingly. "What a terrible mess giving them over to the enemy."

An Earth Alliance destroyer fired on the Aegis. It avoided the volley and in an elegant display of aeronautics, gripped the destroyer's front end, held the Scylla canon firmly between two talons, and launched mortars. Violent explosions tore out from the hull and the destroyer cracked apart.

The Blitz deployed the Mirage Colloid, its black fuselage disappearing as it sped toward another destroyer. It reappeared directly in front of the bridge, fired out a Gleipnir anchor from its left arm, and smashed the deck in two. The Buster dove in after it and hefted both the Launcher and the Rifle attached to its arms. A swift one-two punch: anti-armor followed by a hyper impulse beam. The ship instantly burst open.

The Duel came down the fleet's rear flank, firing its rail guns and canons at a different destroyer. Crimson flames spit from the destroyer's gaping holes—another ship went down. Menelaos' operator announced, "Syracuse hit; incapacitated. The Cassandros is sunk!"

The next operator called out, "Antigonos, Ptolemaios, sunk!"

The color drained from Captain Hoffman's face. "What? After only six minutes? Four ships down?"

"Two ships approaching," the first operator said. "One a Nazca-class and the other a Laurasia-class. Dead ahead!"

"They've locked laser sights on the Syracuse and Cassandros," said the second operator.

"What?!" Admiral Halberton couldn't believe his ears. They were aiming on two completely disabled ships? It was slaughter! "Damn you, Creuset!"

> > > > >

On the Vesalius' bridge, Creuset watched as his mobile suits carved up the fleet. He shook his head. "Athrun and Nicol are naïve if they think we can leave survivors behind."

The main guns of the Vesalius and the Gamow suddenly unleashed fire. A momentary flash of blinding light—two wounded destroyers burst open like fruit. Without pausing, the mobile suits continued to target new ships, one after another. And still, the fleet refused to reform and abandon the Archangel.

Creuset was getting bored. "Halberton thinks he will be able to shield the Paw all the way to Earth. Noble sentiments, though foolish."

Ades replied, "So much the easier for us, especially if they keep the Strike tucked away."

Creuset laughed. "They are quite aware that their battleships and armors cannot beat us. Halberton is sitting on their only hope for survival. Perhaps we need to make that even more clear."

> > > > >

The Archangel's bridge fell silent as the image of the decimated Syracuse and Cassandros appeared on their screens. The intercom on the captain's chair crackled—it was La Flaga. "Hey! Why am I still standing by to launch? We're in trouble with those Gundams out there!"

"Lieutenant," Murrue answered, "we have not been given permission to sortie. Continue to stand by." She knew that he'd worked hard to get the Zero back in perfect order and he was impatient to get moving, but she had orders. And frankly, she wasn't thrilled to think of him out there alone in this kind of fight.

He started shouting and cursing. She switched off the intercom. Murrue sympathized, but her objective was to get the ship and the Strike safely to headquarters. Otherwise, the fleet's sacrifice would be meaningless.

"Murrue!" La Flaga hailed again.

She shut her eyes. Minutes ticked by . . . more and more ships were lost. Murrue couldn't simply stand there and do nothing. She made a swift decision. "Move away from the Menelaos!" she ordered.

The minute the Archangel changed course, Halberton appeared on the monitor. "What are you doing, Ramius?"

"I mean to separate the Archangel from the fleet and start the landing sequence, with your permission, Admiral."

Behind the Admiral, Captain Hoffman scoffed. "You aim to escape alone?"

Glaring, Murrue said, "The enemy is targeting us specifically. As long as we're here, the fleet doesn't stand a chance."

"We'll never make Alaska now," Halberton said. "However, from this position we could at least descend into Earth Force territory. We could shake the GINNs in reentry."

Murrue shook her head. "Your Excellency, I firmly disagree. You must let us go alone!"

A smile broke out on Halberton's face. "You are a very unreasonable woman, Lieutenant Ramius."

She grinned back. "I learned from the best."

"Very well. The Archangel will prepare to land at once. We'll take you as far as the coordinating point, but from there, you're on your own."

> > > > >

"Descend?! In the middle of all this??" La Flaga looked at Officer Murdoch's confused face on his screen. "Maybe I shouldn't have been so hard on her . . ." He looked down for a moment, then put his sarcastic smile carefully back into place. "Well. Better than hanging around here, I guess. This party's a drag."

"Even if we lose the mobile suits, we'd still have to take on three battleships," came a voice behind him.

La Flaga and Murdoch turned around—Kira stood there in his pilot suit.

"Y-you!" Murdoch stammered. Everyone in the hangar was taken aback.

Everyone but La Flaga, it seemed. "What, couldn't stay away?"

"I'll stand by in the Strike," Kira said. "We're still in Number One battle formation, right?"

The Hawk of Endymion smiled, giving Kira a hearty push up toward the Gundam. He continued smiling until the boy climbed into the cockpit, but then his expression grew sullen and dark. "So many battles ahead of you, Kira," he murmured. "You're never gonna be the same."

La Flaga had been younger than Kira when he'd first distinguished himself on the field. He knew this war would change Kira Yamato forever.

> > > > >

Admiral Halberton's voice rang out over a communications channel, "Menelaos to all ships of the Eighth Fleet. Your primary objective is to defend the Archangel at all costs. Hold on until it reaches Earth's atmosphere!" Pausing, the admiral said, "We cannot lose this ship. The future depends on it. Regroup and do not let yourself be outflanked!"

The Archangel began its landing sequence. Moebiuses and GINNs violently entangled, their missiles rushing at each other. Volleys of fire from ZAFT mobile suits pounded the Earth Force's mobile armor cockpits. Most of the Earth Force's machines were blown to bits, but the destroyer ships hacked into the GINNs with their main guns. It looked like fireworks.

> > > > >

The Vesalius sent out a laser communiqué to the X Numbers informing them that the Archangel was trying to descend. Yzak had just demolished two Moebiuses when he got the message. He ground his teeth. "I won't allow it!"

He pushed the Duel through the dense vanguard; the three other Gundams followed close behind. They weaved past the destroyers' main guns, firing rockets at the engines and cutting holes in the broadsides of the ships.

The Menelaos fired its main gun—BOOM. A deep, pulsing red splayed light, but the Gundams just kept on coming.

> > > > >

Kira stood by in the Strike's cockpit. He placed the little girl's paper flower on his console and smiled. It would be his icon; the symbol of all for which he fought.

As the Archangel continued its descent sequence, Officer Chandra shouted from the bridge, "The Duel and the Buster have broken through the lines!"

Kira tensed as Tonomura said, "The Menelaos has engaged in the hostilities."

He radioed the Zero. "La Flaga!"

"I hear it, kid," the pilot responded. He hailed the bridge. "Captain! Get us out there while there's still time!"

Murrue's voice shot back, "What do you mean 'us'?"

Kira gripped his microphone. "According to my specs, it's possible for the Strike to descend into Earth's atmosphere on its own."

"Kira?!?" Murrue and Miriallia overlapped each other in their astonishment.

"What are you *doing* here?" Murrue asked.

He realized then that she had wanted him to leave, to break free of this war. But as long as the people he cared about were in jeopardy, he'd always be right in the middle of it. "The Menelaos is in danger!" he said urgently. "Captain, with your permission . . ."

Murrue hesitated. It wasn't that she doubted his abilities, but if he was wrong, and the Strike couldn't survive reentry, their G Weapon would be lost.

"All right!" Natarle interrupted. "But return by Phase Three. It may look fine by the specs but it's never been done before. There's no telling what could happen. Keep an eye on your altitude at all times!"

"Understood!" Kira called back.

The launch hatch opened below Kira; he could see Earth. It looked like a blue shroud. "I've never seen anything like it before," he murmured to La Flaga over the intercom. "It's a shame it has to be at a time like this."

"Makes two of us, kid," La Flaga said.

Squeezing the levers, Kira shouted, "Kira Yamato, launching!"

The Strike catapulted toward Earth. He groaned under the pull of gravity, struggling to press his foot pedals. Once the system was under his control, he headed toward the fray. An alarm went off as the X102 Duel appeared on the monitor. The Gundam was covered in new weaponry. It bore down on the Strike with its beam saber.

> > > > >

The Menelaos shook under heavy fire as images of destruction sprang up on all its monitors. Operators frantically called out the battle's status:

"The Belgrano is gone!"

"Five minutes until reentry!"

Captain Hoffman shouted, "Admiral, this ship can't take any more damage! We must retreat!"

Halberton shook his head. "Not yet."

The bridge jolted under the Buster's hyper impulse rifle. A communications officer said, "The Strike and the Moebius Zero have launched from the Archangel!"

"What?!" Halberton shot out of his chair.

On the monitor, the Strike's white fuselage glowed. It faced off with the Duel—the two were evenly matched. Only one person could pilot that Gundam with such skill: Kira Yamato.

"Perhaps it *is* your fate," Halberton murmured to himself.

"Laurasia-class ship approaching!" an operator cried. The ZAFT battleship rushed toward them.

> > > > >

On the Vesalius' bridge, Ades leaned forward and shouted, "Gamow! You're too close! What are you doing, Zelman?"

The Gamow moved right into the fleet's front lines. A communications line opened up and the Laurasia-class' captain could be heard through a storm of static: "We've been-follow—this far—pull out—originally—" Zelman's voice was strangely calm. On screen, his face looked . . . serene and determined. "The Archan—without fail."

The communications line cut out.

Ades was aghast. Their failure to capture the Archangel was not Zelman's responsibility. Yet the Gamow plunged toward the special battleship to make the ultimate sacrifice.

Commander Creuset watched the monitor, his expression cold and his posture stiff. Ades shuddered as he watched the Gamow charge, full speed, at the Archangel. Even more horrifying, he glanced back over . . . and Creuset was *smiling*.

> > > > >

Seeing the Gamow headed straight for the Archangel, Halberton ordered the Menelaos to move in between the two ships and keep up a steady stream of fire. The Gamow pressed on, unfalteringly.

La Flaga swung in and deployed his gun barrels, emptying the Zero of all its ammo. The Gamow got badly bruised, but didn't sink. It tumbled forward with unstoppable force. Canons blasting, it struck at the Menelaos. Fire exploded from the hull.

Captain Hoffman got up on his feet. "They're gonna suicide bomb us?"

Admiral Halberton ordered sternly, "Put the refugees into an escape pod at once! Those people made it this far; we won't let them down!"

Hoffman grew even paler.

The Menelaos' main guns pierced the Gamow, causing violent explosions to erupt from the Laurasia-class' side. Both ships resembled bloodied prizefighters, covered in wounds, as they were pulled by the Earth's gravitational force.

Listing badly to one side, the Menelaos' hull was enveloped in crimson flames. Through the heat, an escape pod launched, gaining speed as it hurtled toward Earth. Halberton was slightly relieved. The moon's flagship was sinking, but at least the Heliopolis refugees would survive. Now, the Archangel was on its own.

> > > > >

Murrue watched, frozen in terror, as the two great ships fought each other as they catapulted into the Earth's atmosphere. Their hulls grew red with friction.

Natarle looked at her readings. "Captain! Two minutes until reentry. Ablation shield gel ready to deploy."

"Recall the Zero and the Strike," Murrue snapped.

The Gamow continued forward, thrusting headlong into the Menelaos' starboard side. KA-BOOM! Explosions bellowed from inside the ZAFT vessel. There was a chain reaction; its armor blew completely off. Fragments of the ship blasted into space before disintegrating entirely.

Broken, the Menelaos drifted down, burning brightly—a white-hot glow—then suddenly, quietly, blew apart. Murrue shot to her feet, screaming, "Admiral!" The Menelaos disappeared in white flames . . .

Slowly, she drew her hand back and gave one last salute. Her eyes stung, the blurry image lost as tears ran down her cheeks. "Your Excellency, thank you and farewell."

> > > > >

Athrun heard Nicol's anguished cry over the intercom: "Captain Zelman!"

He watched as the Gamow slammed into the Menelaos and both ships burned up in the atmosphere.

The command to return came over the laser communiqué. Unable to enter the atmosphere without a carrier ship, there was nothing more they could do. Even so, Athrun hesitated, transfixed.

Dive-bombing into the Menelaos served no purpose whatsoever. It didn't help their cause in the slightest.

What a waste. The motives behind such an action gave Athrun a chill. All those people, dead. For what? For *what?*

> > > > >

The Zero shot its anchor into the rear deck of the Archangel and slipped safely inside. The hatch closed behind it and La Flaga jumped out of his cockpit, shouting, "Where's the kid?"

The descent sequence had reached its final stage. On the bridge, the crew hustled through the last minute operations. Over the intercom, Miriallia desperately called for Kira but only white noise answered.

La Flaga ran toward the bridge. "Yo! Anyone seen the kid?"

Officer Neumann shouted, "We're already entering the atmosphere!"

The ace pilot stopped dead in his tracks.

Angling toward Earth, the Archangel emitted a transparent gel from its ejection ports, which coated the hull, dampening the friction somewhat.

> > > > >

The Duel brought its beam saber down on the Strike; Kira deflected it with his shield and pushed back with all his might. Flying backward, the Duel continued to shoot. They flew apart, lit their vernier thrusters, and charged at each other again.

Kira did a spinning kick, smashing the Duel's face down and sending the Gundam spinning. He retreated while the Duel regained composure. On the monitor, he saw the escape pod, which contained the Heliopolis refugees he almost joined, launch from the sinking Menelaos. It flew directly in between the Duel and the Strike.

The Duel's rifle fired.

"NO!" Kira screamed.

Pushing his verniers, he rushed in, extending Strike's hand. He could see the frightened faces peeking out from the pod's windows—he could see the little girl who had given him a flower—he could see her wide eyes.

The rifle beam pierced the escape shuttle. The outer hull cracked and the pod bounced on the atmosphere like a stone skipping along a lake. Flames surrounded the fuselage; pieces of it flew off as the shuttle burned up.

Kira screamed and screamed, banging his fists on the console until they were bloody. The paper flower came loose and floated around the cockpit.

We do what we have to, to protect the ones we love.

> > > > >

"Kira!" Sai and Tolle both shouted in front of their monitors on board the bridge.

"Does he intend to land in that form?" Natarle mumbled.

It was too late to dock the Strike; if they opened the Archangel's hatch, it would burn up. Kira would have to make it to Earth on his own. Pal raised his voice, "The Strike's coming in at a different entry angle! We're going to touch down in completely different zones!"

Miriallia desperately called to the Strike. "Kira! Kira, can you return! Return to the ship now!"

"No use," Natarle told her. "The Strike's propulsion system isn't fast enough."

Silence fell over the bridge. Murrue ordered, "Bring the ship closer. We can use our thrusters and get close enough to catch him!"

Neumann objected, "But then we'll miss our landing point, too!"

"If this ship makes it to Alaska without the Strike, it will be altogether pointless!" she shouted back. "Now move!"

Neumann operated the thrusters. Slowly, the Archangel drew closer to the Strike.

"Calculate the touch down zone," Murrue said to Pal.

"One moment." He hurried to do the math as the Archangel advanced towards the Gundam. "Estimated

landing point is . . ." He gasped. "North Africa!" Everyone froze.

"We'll be landing directly in ZAFT territory."

> > > > >

To Be Continued in Volume 2

>>>>>
Commentary

Sunrise Corporation, Work Department, #9 Studio, Creative work: Shimomura Takaharu

Even if you have to shoplift it, I want you to read this book.

These are the words of the late Tanabe Moichi, founder of Kinokuniya Books, upon opening his store in Osaka, Umeda. I don't want you to misconstrue them, though. Shoplifting is a crime. For certain, you'd be crucified. I'd better stop while I'm ahead. Geez!

The main point is: "When you find something really good—hesitate and you'll regret it." This novel is that kind of "something really good."

This time around, I was advised at great length on setups, etc. Officially, it could probably be said that I grasped the story with both hands. The traditional Gundam stories were put together slap-dash, but this time, the materials and chronology created by setup specialist Mr. Morita Shigeru and writer Mr. Yoshino Hiroyuki couldn't even be crammed into a large binder. Moreover, the manuscript drafts continued to get bigger and bigger, matching the progress of the story.

For example, in the explanations of the plastic models, it's written, "The Aile Striker can be used in water," and, "with the Sword Striker, it performs in big scuffles."

Those types of scenes weren't broadcast on the show, but still they existed. There is no mistake about how intricate this universe is; I say that having written it.

In episode 11, there is a scene where the Duel's and Strike's beam sabers cross. It was shown in a certain magazine, and SEED was written so that that picture didn't turn out to be a big lie. Right during the dubbing work, when Supervisor Fukuda was watching that story play out on screen, only that scene was shown. The two of us fell off our chairs.

What with one problem after another, I read the main draft drenched in a cold sweat. As for this book, Professor Liu Goto corrected it to correspond to its original storyline. How many times have I said I'm sorry to Professor Goto already?

Still. . . Isn't it okay if I made a cool change? Wouldn't a Midas Messer be all right? Isn't the Mirage Colloid wonderful? I'm not evil for deviating from the original! Next time, the Strike will beat that devil Gundam, the Duel, without fail!

With my pretending to be stupid, and telling you so many random stories, I've strayed from my point: This book isn't a shoot-'em-up war novel. As literary media and broadcast media have different methods of presentation, even if they deal with the same subject matter, it's only natural that they'll have different qualities.

I don't want you to misunderstand—I'm not saying that this novel is really different from the world of SEED that's being broadcast on TV. For example, if there are cases where a battle scene that spends several pages in print lacks the impact of two seconds of imagery, there are also cases where the psychological descriptions of the characters that mope across the screen for a moment can't be captured in just one line of monologue.

When I met with Professor Goto last winter, we talked about these differences. This time we agreed that we should give equal attention and weight to each character.

The professor said he especially liked Tolle. I liked L-chan, [Lacus] but I couldn't say that, because it would be a problem if people thought I was a pervert. It goes without saying, but a Lolita Complex is not an illness. It's just a *hobby*. (I'm normal. I've even been married. Once. But I digress.)

While eating with the voice actors after an episode's recording, we talked about all kinds of things. Everybody had their own takes on their parts and they were worried about what would happen to them. (Specifically, they were worried that this was a Gundam series where characters die left and right. At first, the supervisor made Mr. Hoshiso Ichiro cry when he said, "Don't think you're going to survive until the end, just because you're playing the main character." It's the first time I've heard a supervisor threaten a voice actor.)

Mr. Takato Yasuhiro, who plays Pal and Kuzzey, spoke to me for more than ten minutes straight about his warm feelings for Kuzzey, and Mr. Shiratori Tetsu, who plays Sai, said: "Lately, [around episode 22] I'm finding it hard to look Mr. Hoshi in the face (without laughing)." And Miss Shindoh Naomi, who plays Cagalli, proved that Mr. Nishikawa "Miguel" Takanori looked just like his mother.

But let's return to the story. I've been feeling schizophrenic lately.

This time, besides Sunrise's sales department people talking seriously with someone from Kadokawa Publishing, I was chatting foolishly with the friendly neighborhood news and also the stupid news sources. The Professor came back from a day trip to Nagoya, and despite the fact that he was tired, he smiled at this easily flattered person whom he met for the first time. Afterwards, I greatly regretted it.

Kira and Athrun . . . Kira and Lacus . . . Lacus and Athrun . . . Hawk and Le Creuset . . . A web of various complex relationships is constructed in SEED. Even in the middle of this book, (in which we still haven't even gotten to episode 13) Kira, Athrun, Flay, and the rest are already advancing such that we can't predict their own fate. What kinds of things are they thinking about, on the inside?

The audience watching the broadcast has to imagine the character's inner lives. Or possibly I'm letting *my* imagination run wild, and maybe they don't even enjoy the anime? Is it like a one-sided love letter? How nice—*one-sided.* I love that word.

Anyway, this book may become one of the guidelines to help fans understand the characters' inner workings. I say guideline, because well, despite the fact that I've written it conceitedly, even *I* can't really imagine the inner workings of Kira and Athrun.

On the birthday of the woman I fell in love with at first sight, I said to her, "I want to give a present to a girl the same age as you, so choose it with me," and so I got her to come shopping with me. The next day, I suddenly gave her the gift we'd chosen and a bouquet of about fifty roses; my point: I can be a decidedly charming idiot, see?

So read this book and diligently study its subtle psychology. It came after the anime, but both fans of SEED and fans of Professor Goto's materials can enjoy this book's contents. The broadcast will break into "Gundam vs. Gundam" wars again. Before then hadn't you better read the novel and review it?

The next book will be "Desert Tiger," set in Bartfeld. Please wait for it!

Oh, yes, this year I'm going to give that girl I love so much a Haro that talks with Mitsuishi's voice! (laughs)

> > > > >
Gundam Glossary

Alaska - The location of the central headquarters for the Earth Alliance Force.

Beam Saber - A new kind of weapon first engaged by the Gundam prototypes of the Earth Alliance Force. Beam blasts are effective even against Phase Shift Armor, but repeated use will drain the energy battery of the mobile suits.

Belgrano - An escort ship that is armed only with three inch vulcan cannons, missile launchers, and torpedo tubes. It has no internal storage for mobile suits.

Bloody Valentine - On February 14th, Cosmic Era 70, only three days after the declaration of war between the Naturals and the Coordinators, the Earth Alliance attacked the PLANT known as Junius Seven. Secret nuclear missiles that were housed aboard the mobile armor carrier called Roosevelt destroyed it. Over 243,000 civilian inhabitants were massacred. The tragedy became a battle cry for young Coordinators who joined the ZAFT forces.

Blue Cosmos - The most radical of the anti-Coordinator activist groups formed by Naturals. The Blue Cosmos ideology says that genetic modification is a violation of the natural order and Coordinators must be exterminated so as to preserve the natural world.

CE - Cosmic Era.

Central Axial Shaft - Provides structural support to the satellite colony of Heliopolis.

Coordinator - A person with mental and physical abilities that have been enhanced by genetic engineering.

Elecar - A fully automated electronic car that provides public transportation for the citizens of the colony Heliopolis.

Evidence 01 - A mysterious fossil discovered by George Gleen, the first Coordinator, inside an asteroid in the vicinity of Europa, one of Jupiter's moons, in CE 22. The skeleton preserved within the fossil resembles that of a winged whale and is seemingly proof of the existence of extraterrestrial life. This finding served to undermine the authority of the religious leaders who had spearheaded the opposition to genetic modification, and thus indirectly led to public acceptance of Coordinators. The fossil itself is currently located inside the PLANTs Supreme Council building at Aprilius One, the capital city of the PLANTs.

Gamow - The Laurasia-class frigate that serves as an escort for the Vesalius and later becomes the mothership of the captured Duel, Buster, and Blitz Gundams.

GAT-X - A line of prototype mobile suits developed by the Atlantic Federation. They bear the designation Gressorial Armament Tactical-eXperimental, meaning, they can adapt to walk. The designations on the machines indicate in which series their structural frame belongs. They are also known as Gundams.

Gleipnir -The offensive shield system on the Blitz Gundam.

Gottfried - An energy beam cannon on the Archangel.

Gundam - A nickname for the advanced GAT-X series mobile suits. It stands for, "General Unilateral Neuro-link Dispersive Autonomic Maneuver" system.

Heliopolis - A resource satellite controlled by the Orb Union, one of Earth's neutral nations. Heliopolis uses a traditional Island 3 space colony design, reinforced with a central axial shaft. The colony cylinder is attached to a mining asteroid. The mine serves as a source of raw materials. Heliopolis is officially neutral territory, making it an attractive refuge for families like those of Kira Yamato and his friends who hope to avoid being drawn into the current conflict. However, Heliopolis has secretly been playing host to the Atlantic Federation's Gundam project and thus lending support to the Earth Alliance.

Igelstellung - A computer-controlled multi-barrel vulcan gun. A close-in weapons system (CIWS) designed for shooting down missiles and aircraft at short ranges. It can be used against infantry and other ground targets. It can also be used as a defense weapon against enemy mobile suits.

Junius Seven - The seventh of the Junius City PLANTs. It was destroyed in the Bloody Valentine incident. One of the only PLANTs allowed by the Naturals to produce food, it was converted into an agricultural production facility in 60 CE to help the PLANTs attain self-sufficiency.

Menelaos - A warship designed as a carrier that can quickly deploy large numbers of mobile armors. It is of the Agamemnon class.

Mobile armor - Earth Alliance's one-man, general-purpose, heavy fighter used as the standard combat vehicle. It is designed to provide maximum effectiveness so that the loss of skilled personnel is minimized.

Mobile suits - Mobile suits are the humanoid fighting vehicles, in other words, giant robots that are the standard weapon of warfare in the Gundam saga. Mobile suits typically range in size from 15 to 25 meters (50 to 80 feet), and are usually operated by a single human pilot. Their versatility and precise maneuverability make them superior to any conventional tank or space fighter.

Montgomery - A warship that is heavily armed and equipped with an internal storage bay for mobile suits. It is also a flagship of the Eighth Fleet that comes to meet the Archangel.

Morgenroete Inc. - A semi-nationalized munitions company based in the Orb Union, which also maintains facilities at the resource satellite Heliopolis. Although its primary clients are the armed forces of the neutral nation Orb, Morgenroete has been secretly collaborating with the Atlantic Federation on its

Gundam development projects and on the construction of the warship Archangel.

Orb Union - An island nation in the southern Pacific Ocean. It possesses industrial and military power and has highly advanced technology, an abundant supply of geothermal energy, and a policy of nondiscrimination against Coordinators.

PLANT Colonies - Productive Location Ally on Nexus Technology have become a new homeland for Coordinators fleeing the persecution they experienced on Earth. As their name suggests, the PLANTs were created to serve as research and manufacturing sites, but their unique design also enables them to recreate a lush natural environment, with abundant vegetation and open water.

Port of Artemis - An asteroid fortress controlled by the Eurasian Federation. Considered a backwater base of little strategic value, oddly enough, its umbrella defense shield makes it virtually impenetrable.

Phase Shift - The most distinctive feature of the prototype Gundams developed by the Atlantic Federation. While active, this special armor nullifies all attacks by physical weapons, including blades, projectiles, and conventional explosives. However, it has no effect against beam and laser weapons, so most of the Gundams also carry shields treated with anti-beam coating. And because Phase Shift Armor consumes large amounts of energy, it cannot be used for extended periods lest it drain the mobile suit's energy battery. Phase Shift Armor changes color upon activation. The Gundams that use this technology sport brilliant colors while in their Active Mode, and turn a dull gray when they switch to De-activated Mode.

Schwert Gewehr - A 15.78m anti-ship blade on the GAT-X105 Sword Strike Gundam.

Umbrella of Artemis - The lightwave defense barrier that protects the Eurasian Federation's Artemis military base. It is impenetrable to physical and energy weapons, but the barrier is only activated when there are enemies in the area.

Vernier engines - Secondary rockets on mobile suits used for changing directions and performing intricate movements. Also called an apogee motor.

Vesalius - The Nazca-class high-speed destroyer that serves as Creuset's flagship. This is ZAFT's newest model of warship; armed with powerful beam cannons, it is faster than the Archangel.

X Number mobile suits (G Weapons; Gundams) - Five Earth Alliance mobile suits built in secrecy on Heliopolis.

ZAFT - (Zodiac Alliance of Freedom Treaty.) ZAFT is a militia made up of civilian volunteers, and the organization has no formal rank structure, so its members are instead addressed by descriptive titles like "commander" and "captain." Since ZAFT membership is made up of genetically enhanced Coordinators, its forces are more than a match for the numerically superior Earth Alliance. (ZAFT was originally a political organization called the Zodiac Alliance, which was founded in CE 50 by Siegel Clyne and Patrick Zala. The Zodiac Alliance took on its present name in CE 65, and three years later it was reorganized to become an explicitly military organization equipped with the revolutionary new weapons known as mobile suits.) The ZAFT forces are currently subject to the authority of the PLANT Supreme Council and report directly to the National Defense Committee, chaired by Patrick Zala.

Zodiac - A research colony that hosted the investigation of the extraterrestrial fossil. The research organization grew into space's largest research facility and became a thriving center for space science.

> > > > >
Coming Soon

The Archangel managed to evade Creuset's force and successfully descended to Earth, but they were set off their original course for the Atlantic Federation Headquarters in Alaska. Instead, they end up in North Africa, in the heart of ZAFT territory. The infamous ZAFT commander, Andrew Waltfeld (known as the deadly "Desert Tiger,") stands between the Archangel and escape. Kira's superb Coordinator skills in operating the Gundam Strike once again prove invaluable to his Natural friends. In the exciting second volume of GUNDAM SEED, more is revealed about the true origins of the Coordinators, the identity of the mysterious girl Kira met on Heliopolis, and the budding relationship between Kira and Flay.

TOKYOPOP SHOP

DRAMACON™

Sometimes even two's a crowd.

When Christie settles in the Artist Alley of her first-ever anime convention, she only sees it as an opportunity to promote the comic she has started with her boyfriend. But conventions are never what you expect, and soon a whirlwind of events sweeps Christie off her feet and changes her life. Who is the mysterious cosplayer that won't even take off his sunglasses indoors? What do you do when you fall in love with a guy who is going to be miles away from you in just a couple of days?

CREATED BY SVETLANA CHMAKOVA, CREATOR OF MANGA-STYLE ONLINE COMICS "CHASING RAINBOWS" AND "NIGHT SILVER"!

Preview the manga at:
www.TOKYOPOP.com/dramacon

NO LOITERING

TEEN
AGE 13+